E JOHNSON · JEFF GORDON
RRELL WALTRIP · TONY STEW
ERB THOMAS · TIM FLOCK · NED JARRET
N · BILL ELLIOTT · KYLE LARSON · RICHA
N · JEFF GORDON · LEE PETTY · DAVID
ALTRIP · TONY STEWART · JOEY LOGANO
AS · TIM FLOCK · NED JARRETT · KYLE B
T · KYLE LARSON · RICHARD PETTY · DA
ON · LEE PETTY · DAVID PEARSON · CAL
EWART · JOEY LOGANO · BUCK BAKER · J
NED JARRETT · KYLE BUSCH · RED BYRON
ON · RICHARD PETTY · DALE EARNHARDT
Y · DAVID PEARSON · CALE YARBOROUGH
LOGANO · BUCK BAKER · JOE WEATHERLY
· KYLE BUSCH · RED BYRON · BOBBY ALL
TTY · DALE EARNHARDT · JIMMIE JOHNS
N · CALE YARBOROUGH · DARRELL WALT
ER · JOE WEATHERLY · HERB THOMAS · T
YRON · BOBBY ALLISON · BILL ELLIOTT ·
OT · JIMMIE JOHNSON · JEFF GORDON · L
H · DARRELL WALTRIP · TONY STEWART ·

I0818476

The IMMORTALS *of* NASCAR

43

The IMMORTALS of NASCAR

Andrew Clarke

A Gelding Street Press book
An imprint of Rockpool Publishing
PO Box 252
Summer Hill
NSW 2130 Australia

geldingstreetpress.com
Follow us! @ Geldingstreet_press

ISBN: 9781922662354

Published in 2026 by Gelding Street Press

Copyright text © Andrew Clarke 2026
Copyright design © Rockpool Publishing 2026

Front cover & p.ii: The King: seven-time Cup Series champion Richard Petty at the start of the Daytona 500 on February 17, 1980. (Robert Alexander/Archive Photos/Getty Images)

Back cover: Racing underway at the Daytona Beach and Road Course in 1956, a stone's throw from where NASCAR began. (Alamy)

Endpapers: Red Byron, the first Immortal of NASCAR. (ISC Archives/CQ-Roll Call Group via Getty Images)

Design and typesetting by Christine Armstrong, Rockpool Publishing
Edited by Brooke Halliwell

All rights reserved. No part of this publication may be reproduced, stored in a retrieval system, or transmitted in any form or by any means, electronic, mechanical, photocopying, recording or otherwise, without the prior written permission of the publisher.

A catalogue record for this book is available from the National Library of Australia

Printed and bound in China

10 9 8 7 6 5 4 3 2 1

Dedication

To my family, who first taught me the meaning of passion in sport.

To the friends and colleagues who encouraged me to chase stories worth telling, and those who opened doors for me.

To the drivers, crews, and fans whose courage and character made NASCAR what it is, and whose voices echo through every lap of history.

This book is for those who inspired me to love the sport, to honor its legends, and to keep their stories alive.

Contents

Foreword by Richard Petty

When people ask me about the history of NASCAR, I tell them the story always comes back to one thing – the drivers. You can have the fastest car, the best engine, the smartest crew chief, but at the end of the day, it's the person behind the wheel who makes the difference. That's what built this sport. That's what grew it from a handful of stock cars on dirt tracks to a national spectacle watched by millions.

I was lucky. I was born into it. My daddy, Lee Petty, ran the very first NASCAR race in 1949. He was probably the first true professional in our sport – he made his living strictly from racing, back when that meant buying a car for $1,000 and hoping to win $1,500 on the weekend. He raced smart, didn't tear up his stuff, and finished races. They called him "Mr Consistency," and he passed that mindset down to me.

As a kid, I watched men like Red Byron, Tim Flock, and Glenn "Fireball" Roberts start something without even realizing how big it would become. I always admired Tim Flock – he was smooth, smart, and always found a way to win. Later, I raced against the next wave: Joe Weatherly, Ned Jarrett, and David Pearson. Guys who all brought something special. Weatherly was wild – on the track and off – but he had heart. Ned was a gentleman racer, calm and consistent. And Pearson? He might have been the most naturally gifted of us all. I probably finished second to him more than anyone else.

In my own time, I saw the sport evolve and so did the drivers. Cale Yarborough was one of the toughest sons of guns I ever raced. He didn't know how to back off. He was driving hard, no matter what lap it was. Bobby Allison was relentless. Darrell Waltrip came in with flash and fire, said what he thought, and raced just as bold. And then came Dale Earnhardt – the Intimidator. He was rough around the edges, didn't care what people thought, but he had that fire in him. That's what connected him with the fans. That, and seven championships.

Each generation had its standard bearer. Pearson carried us through the '60s and '70s. I had my run. Dale brought a new grit and attitude. Jeff Gordon

Seven-time NASCAR Cup champion Richard Petty. (ISC Images & Archives via Getty Images)

brought youth and polish. Jimmie Johnson? He just went out and won – quietly, methodically, with class. And now we've got the likes of Kyle Busch, Joey Logano, and Kyle Larson, all fierce in different ways, all pushing the boundaries of talent and technology.

The Immortals of NASCAR aren't just the men who won the most races or lifted the most trophies. They're the ones who defined eras, carried the sport on their shoulders, and brought fans to the track week after week. They made you cheer – or made you boo – but they always made you care.

I've been fortunate to race against many of these men. I've been lucky enough to win a few, lose a lot, and witness the growth of something bigger than any of us ever imagined. NASCAR started as a Southern sport with guys wrenching on their own cars in dirt-floor garages. Now it's a global brand. But no matter how much it grows, the driver will always be at the center of it.

Because the car doesn't become legendary until someone drives it like it was never meant to be driven.

That's what these Immortals did. And that's why they'll never be forgotten.

Richard Petty
Level Cross, North Carolina

Top: The south turn at Daytona Beach and Road Course coming onto the beach during the 1948 race at Daytona. (ISC Archives/CQ-Roll Call Group via Getty Images)

Bottom: Red Byron (left), NASCAR's first "Cup Series" champion and the first Immortal, with NASCAR founder "Big" Bill France (right). (ISC Images & Archives via Getty Images)

Introduction: From stock cars to NASCAR & immortality

More than 3,000 drivers have started a NASCAR race in its 75-year history. Around 200 have won a race. Just 36 have claimed the championship trophy. Yet only 20 are being named Immortals in this book – an elite group whose feats transcend the win columns and trophy cabinets.

NASCAR is the second-biggest motorsport in the world, behind only Formula 1, and the second-most-watched sport in America, trailing only the NFL. It's a phenomenon born in the dusty paddocks and red clay ovals of the Southern Piedmont region, fueled by ego, grit, and moonshine, and it grew into a billion-dollar empire of noise, steel, and personality.

What began as a local curiosity among moonshine runners – drivers who could outrun the law in stripped-down Ford V-8s – soon became a cultural juggernaut. Racing wasn't just about speed; it was about reputation, survival, and pride. The Depression had flattened the South, and young men with fast cars and no money saw the racetrack as a way out.

Those early days were chaotic. Events were run on dirt ovals in county fairgrounds and cow paddocks. Promoters stiffed drivers, rules changed by the week, and crashes were plentiful. But the crowds kept coming. They came for the action, the danger, and the brawls in the infield that followed spectacular crashes and bitter rivalries.

Daniel S. Pierce nailed it in his book *Real NASCAR*: "They came to watch their heroes maneuver ordinary automobiles at incredible speed, beating and banging on each other, wrecking spectacularly, and fighting out their differences in the infield."

Fighting. Feuding. Wrecking. Winning. It was – and is – the DNA of NASCAR.

Then came Bill France Sr., a racer who saw that the sport needed structure to thrive. He organized it, tamed it just enough to sell it, and then turned it into a national pastime. France was never the fastest driver, but he was the sport's most important figure. His founding of the

More than 80 cars lined up in front of 28,000 fans for the 1955 NASCAR race on the 4.2-mile Daytona Beach and Road Course, but with the series' popularity exploding, it would soon outgrow the place where its roots were planted in the late 1930s. (ISC Archives/CQ-Roll Call Group via Getty Images)

National Association for Stock Car Auto Racing – NASCAR – on February 21, 1948 at the Streamline Hotel in Daytona lit the match for everything that followed.

But our list of Immortals is not about the promoters or the businessmen. It's about the drivers. The ones who made fans scream, sponsors sign checks, and rivals seethe. This is not just a list of champions. It is a tribute to those whose presence altered the course of the sport – on the track and beyond it.

Richard Petty. Dale Earnhardt. Jimmie Johnson. These seven-time champions are the sport's holy trinity: The King, The Intimidator, and JJ. Each represents

Fighting. Feuding. Wrecking. Winning. It was – and is – the DNA of NASCAR.

a different generation, a different style, but the same relentless pursuit of greatness.

But greatness doesn't only wear the crown. Red Byron raced with a war-shattered leg. Darrell Waltrip transformed NASCAR's voice as much as its tactics. Tim Flock had a monkey riding shotgun. And modern icons like Kyle Busch, Joey Logano, and Kyle Larson – each still chasing more titles – have helped redefine what it means to be a NASCAR star in the 21st century.

We tell their stories not because they won the most, but because they left something behind that will outlast them.

To understand NASCAR's heartbeat, you need to understand its roots. The Southern Piedmont region – a crescent stretching from central Virginia, through the Carolinas to Georgia and Alabama – was NASCAR's original proving ground. A land of rebels, racers, and redemption. Modified Fords became stock cars, and outlaws became icons.

The first season of what we now call the NASCAR Cup Series was launched in 1949 as the Strictly Stock Division. It became the Grand National Series in 1950, then rebranded to the Winston Cup Series in 1971 when Big Tobacco money rolled in. Nextel took over in 2004, which evolved into the Sprint Cup in 2008. Then came the Monster Energy era, and finally, the modern era without a sponsor and *just* the NASCAR Cup Series in 2020. We've used the era-appropriate terms throughout the book to mark each driver's time.

What hasn't changed, though, is the spectacle.

From the early days of bootleggers and bar fights, NASCAR transitioned to a national obsession. Through the '60s and '70s, paved superspeedways replaced dusty bullrings, and stars like Petty, Bobby Allison, Yarborough, and Pearson became part of American folklore.

The 1979 Daytona 500 changed everything. Cale Yarborough and Donnie Allison wrecked on the final lap. Bobby Allison pulled over. Helmets flew, punches landed, and a national TV audience fell in love. NASCAR wasn't just a Southern thing anymore, but an American thing.

By the 1990s, NASCAR's reach had grown coast to coast. Jeff Gordon brought a new, polished style. Dale Earnhardt brought fire. The two of them gave the sport a storyline for the ages. As NASCAR surged into the 2000s, it began appearing in new markets – Las Vegas, Los Angeles, Chicago – and on every media platform imaginable.

While TV ratings have fluctuated and some tracks have fallen away, NASCAR remains a cultural force. The Next Gen car has brought parity. Street circuits and road courses now mix with short tracks and superspeedways. International stars – like Shane Van Gisbergen – are helping introduce the sport to new audiences.

It's important to remember that NASCAR never had the global ambitions of F1, but it is adapting. Canada. Mexico. Europe. Even Australia and New Zealand are watching more closely now. And as new fans arrive, they'll need heroes to follow. This book introduces them to the Immortals.

The start of a race at the beginning of the NASCAR Modified season, 1949. (ISC Images & Archives via Getty Images)

They came for the action, the danger, and the brawls in the infield that followed spectacular crashes and bitter rivalries.

And before the Immortals came, there was *Big Bill.*

William France Sr. is the man who made all of this possible. After racing himself, he saw the need for a governing body. He saw that fans would pay if they could see the best. He saw that drivers needed protection and promotion. And he saw that NASCAR could be a business.

His first race as a driver at Daytona in 1936 ended in chaos. Soft sand. Broken cars. Lost money. But France returned, organized more races, and eventually founded NASCAR. He built the Daytona International Speedway. He strong-armed sponsors. He unified teams. He turned a regional curiosity into a national colossus.

France's family still runs the sport. And while he doesn't qualify for our list of Immortals – this is for drivers only – he earns a special mention as the *pre-Immortal.* Without Big Bill, there would be no NASCAR as we know it.

And from those beach races came the sport we know today: high banks, roaring crowds, emotional victories, and

There are 13 champions in this 1996 photo, with 50 titles between them. (Alamy)

devastating crashes. Heroes are born in moments. Legends are born in seasons. *Immortals* are born when the moments never fade.

For this book, we have ordered the list by the number of titles in descending order, followed by date of birth in ascending order – aside from Kyle Larson, who won his second title after this book had gone to print. At least the win confirmed his immortality. But for people like Red Byron, who appears towards the end, this is not meant to diminish his achievements, I have a photo hanging on my wall with the inscription "The First Immortal," which in many ways he was. Some of those early drivers could have won a lot more if they'd been able to start racing at a younger age.

Three key voices helped shape this book through interviews in February 2025. Richard Petty, the seven-time champion known as "The King," also contributed the foreword. Richard Childress, former driver and the team owner behind Dale Earnhardt's six titles, remains one of NASCAR's wisest figures. And Drew Brown, a veteran PR and media man since the 1980s, brought decades of insight from working closely with many of the sport's modern greats.

Richard Petty with his trophy for winning the Lone Star 500, 1972. (Alamy)

Richard Petty

Birth date	July 2, 1937
Place of birth	Level Cross, North Carolina
Cup Series titles	7 (1964, 1967, 1971, 1972, 1974, 1975, 1979)
Competed between	1958–1992
Results	200 wins from 1,185 races

He is known as "The King," which gives you some idea of the place in which Richard Petty stands in NASCAR history. The stats, however compelling, tell only part of the story. The secret sauce is the thing no one can define. Charisma. Presence. Connection. He had it all to go with a set of stats that feel like they'll never be bettered.

Like so many sporting greats, Richard Petty carries an unmistakable presence. Even now, nearing his 90s, his arrival commands attention – rooms quieten, eyes turn. Towering in stature with large, calloused hands and a warm, easy smile, he's impossible to miss. The black Stetson, trimmed with feathers and a bold medallion, has become part of his legend – even if it arrived later in the story.

There's a Southern courtesy in his manner; a politeness rooted in upbringing and tradition. Stories about Petty always circle back to his humility and integrity – values that he lived, not just spoke. He wasn't just a driver; he was a bridge between eras, between fans and the track. No one has raced longer, and no one's numbers come close.

During the 1960s and '70s, Richard Petty wasn't just a star in motorsport – he was one of America's most recognizable athletes. Even those who didn't follow racing were familiar with his name. He became a millionaire through the sport at a time when that truly meant something, and long

Richard Petty at the Goodwood Festival of Speed in 2006. (Alamy)

before big money was guaranteed in NASCAR. Not bad for a kid who grew up in a modest home in Level Cross, North Carolina, without electricity or running water.

He might've worn the cowboy hat like a crown and signed every autograph with a smile, but make no mistake – Richard Petty was a racer to his core, just like his father. And like every name in this book, he earned his place through grit, not gimmicks.

He might've had more polish than his old man – more charm, more time for the fans – but don't take that for softness. Richard Petty never chased the spotlight. He chased wins. And he got them. Two hundred of them. No one else has come close. The next name on the list is still nearly a hundred victories behind – a gap that says everything.

As for championships? He collected seven. Not that he ever talked about the numbers. For Petty, titles were just what happened when you won enough races. They were a byproduct of the real goal – being first to the flag.

Racing was always in the blood. His father, Lee, was a three-time champion. His son, Kyle, found success of his own. And his grandson, Adam, looked destined to carry the name even further before his life was tragically cut short in a practice crash at New Hampshire in 2000.

The Pettys weren't just a racing family – they were NASCAR's first royal bloodline. A dynasty. But for Richard, the man they called "The King," it was never about the crown.

It was always about the craft.

From his earliest years, Petty grew up around stock car racing. He worked on cars in the garage next to the family home with his father and brother, Maurice, and raced lower categories as soon as possible, although details of what and how are sketchy. He had to wait until 21 to debut in both the Convertible and Grand National Series.

"I never thought about doing anything else," he says when asked when he knew he was going to race cars. "When I was growing up, my brother and I worked in the shop and did whatever my dad wanted us to do. Daddy was winning races and championships, and for a long time, you never thought about him growing old or quitting racing, because he didn't look that far ahead.

"I always liked to work on cars. I asked Dad if I could race when I got old enough, or when I thought I was old enough. I was 18, and he said, 'Come back when you're 21'. He did the right thing for me."

Richard Petty was a racer to his core, just like his father.

Richard Petty made his Grand National debut 16 days after turning 21, in the 1958 Jim Mideon 500 in Toronto – a race won by his father, Lee, who even used his front bumper to move his son aside while lapping him. Petty ran nine races that year, earning $760, while Lee won over $9,000 and his second title.

By 1959, Petty started 21 of 44 races and was named Rookie of the Year. The following season marked his breakout. Switching to Plymouth and adopting the now-iconic #43, he won three times – including a clever, calculated pass for victory on the dirt at Charlotte that revealed his racing IQ.

He led the points at times but was ultimately second to Rex White. Still, he'd arrived. He led 447 laps, earned over $40,000, and proved that if he kept winning, the money would take care of itself.

Richard was thrust into the spotlight in 1961 after a crash nearly ended his father's career. Both Pettys crashed during the Daytona qualifying races, but while Richard was quickly

Richard Petty remains active in and around NASCAR. In 2025, he recorded a podcast and YouTube show after each NASCAR race with his former crew chief, Dale Inman, in the lounge of the Petty family home. (Andrew Clarke)

released, Lee suffered serious injuries that sidelined him for 14 months. He returned briefly but raced only six more times before retiring.

It was a tough season for Richard, with just two wins and a drop to eighth in the standings. Still, the 1959 switch to Plymouth was paying off. While Ford and GM dominated the sport and fan allegiances, Petty and Plymouth carved out their own niche.

"In those days, you had Ford people and Chevrolet people," Petty explained. "Then you had us. If your Chevy wasn't going to win, you sure weren't pulling for a Ford – you pulled for me."

By 1962, he was voted NASCAR's Most Popular Driver for the first time. And as he liked to remind people, he won in seven different makes of cars – proof, he said, of the talent behind Petty Enterprises. That included his brother Maurice on engines and cousin Dale Inman calling the shots. They knew how to adapt. And they knew how to win.

Petty's career is too long and has too many wins to go through in detail in these pages, and strangely, there is little that has been written about him aside from a few minimal biographies, some of which are little more than essays, and his autobiography in 1971.

In 1962 and 1963, Petty finished runner-up to Joe Weatherly in the championship. He claimed eight wins from 52 starts and the Most Popular Driver award in '62, then followed with 14 wins from 54 races in '63 – but Weatherly had mastered the art of points racing. That year, he drove for nine different teams, including Petty Enterprises, in his pursuit of the title.

In 1964, Chrysler rolled out its powerful new Hemi engine, and Petty made it count. He won nine races, captured his first championship, and became just the second driver to earn over $100,000 in a single NASCAR season. That year also saw his first Daytona 500 victory – by a full lap, having led 184 of 200 circuits.

Weatherly, his main rival, was tragically killed early in the season. But Petty's dominance was such that it's unlikely even Weatherly could have challenged him. He wrapped up the year with a 40,252 to 34,950 points margin over Ned Jarrett, despite Jarrett winning six more races.

NASCAR banned the Plymouth Belvedere and its 426 Hemi engine for 1965, caving to pressure from Ford and GM. In protest, Chrysler boycotted the season – and took its biggest star with it. Petty briefly switched to drag racing, driving a Hemi-powered Barracuda with "OUTLAWED" painted on the door. But tragedy struck in Dallas, Georgia, when he lost control and crashed into the crowd, killing eight-year-old Wayne Dye.

Even to this day, fans bring their cars to "Petty's Garage" in Level Cross for modifications, signatures, and photographs. (Andrew Clarke)

The Dye family sued the track, Petty Enterprises, and Chrysler. According to Petty's autobiography, *King Richard I*, they

In 1975, Richard Petty won the NASCAR Cup Series points title amid a revamped system: for the first time in series history, each race on the schedule awarded an equal number of points for the winner. (ISC Archives/CQ-Roll Call Group via Getty Images)

settled out of court, paying the family more than the track had earned that year. "Nothing in my life ever hit me like that," Petty wrote. "I tried going back to drag racing, but I couldn't stop thinking about the boy. So I quit."

Desperate to get its biggest star back, NASCAR struck a deal with Chrysler to bring Petty and a modified Hemi engine back to the track mid-season. He returned to run 14 races – and won four of them.

In 1966, Petty ran 39 of 49 races, taking eight wins, including his second Daytona 500, becoming the first driver to win it twice. He missed some starts after tearing a ligament in his left hand playing backyard football with the crew. He still raced – and won – before undergoing surgery.

The 1966 car was special, but the 1967 model wasn't clicking for Petty, so the team got creative. They mounted the '67 body onto the '66 chassis, and with that one move, Petty went on an unprecedented tear. He won 27 races that season, including 10 straight from Winston-Salem in August to North

Wilkesboro in October, and secured the championship. No one has matched that level of dominance since.

Though Chrysler was once again feuding with NASCAR, Petty kept racing, even when asked to sit out select events. This era also marked the rise of specialized cars for different tracks. While Petty had alternatives, he stuck with his favorite – a car he called "our pet" – and kept winning.

Of course, what goes up must come down. He still won 16 races in 1968 but only finished third in points. Ten more wins came in 1969, then 18 in 1970 – but still no title. That changed in 1971, when 21 wins earned him his third championship. He backed it up in 1972 to become the first four-time champion.

He was now clearly NASCAR's most popular driver – friendly, accessible, and fiercely competitive. He won his third Daytona 500 just weeks after having 40 percent of his stomach removed, a feat that only added to his legend.

Even four titles weren't the end. He added championships in 1974 and 1975, then finished runner-up two years in a row before recording his first winless season since becoming a full-timer in 1960. Undeterred, Petty claimed his seventh and final championship in 1979

Richard Petty looks into the interior of his race car at a racetrack in Randleman, North Carolina in 1967. (Flip Schulke/Getty Images)

Petty before the Nascar Winston Cup Daytona 500 race at Daytona International Speedway, February 19, 1984. (Focus on Sport/Getty Images)

– even as the wins began to slow for the now-veteran King.

In 1992, he retired … kind of.

"My problem was that I loved to drive race cars. Whether winning or losing, I loved to be in the race car. I think it's the only time that I could kind of control myself – turn here, turn there, put on brakes. I was able to make the decision. That's the only situation that I've ever been in, or felt like I was in any control."

He says he never looked at his career as anything other than "just my life."

"As far as I was concerned, my job was to drive a race car and make a living for my family. If that was your destiny and your fate, and that's the way you got to go with it. But you still have to deliver," which is exactly what he did.

Petty's final win came in the 1984 mid-season race at Daytona. Eight years later, he stepped away with 200 victories and the most decorated career in NASCAR history. But the road to greatness wasn't paved solely with checkered flags.

The sport he helped define was brutal at times. In the 1970 Rebel 400 at Darlington, his Plymouth Road Runner blew a tire and slammed into the pit wall. The car flipped violently, leaving Petty with a serious shoulder injury and handing the title advantage to Bobby Isaac. Worse, his helmet struck the pavement multiple times – an incident that helped prompt NASCAR to mandate the now-standard Petty-designed window net.

Disaster struck again in 1980 at Pocono. Petty crashed heavily in turn two, nearly flipped, and broke his neck – yet still suited up to race the very next weekend at Talladega.

But even away from the track, tragedy followed. In 2000, Petty's grandson, Adam, was killed in a practice crash. For all the wins and glory, Richard Petty's story is also one of resilience – of withstanding what racing can take away.

"Richard was incredible," says Drew Brown. "I worked at RPM [Richard Petty Motorsport] and got to spend real time with him. He's got this image – the glasses, the hat – but the man is incredibly well-read. He can talk politics, economics, history – you name it.

"I remember walking through Manhattan with him for a media appearance. Everyone recognized him. They didn't say his name – they just called out, 'King!' That's when it hit me. He's bigger than just a driver."

"The Intimidator," Dale Earnhardt was as fierce a competitor as NASCAR has ever seen. Some saw him as dirty, but to him, "rubbing was racing" and his craft took him to seven titles. (Alamy)

Dale Earnhardt

Birth date	April 29, 1951; died February 18, 2001
Place of birth	Kannapolis, North Carolina
Cup Series titles	7 (1980, 1986, 1987, 1990, 1991, 1993, 1994)
Competed between	1975–2001
Results	76 wins from 676 races

There are many fans who, to this day, believe NASCAR died on February 18, 2001 when a man nicknamed "The Intimidator" drew his last breath. The crash that claimed the life of Dale Earnhardt concluded one of the most remarkable careers in NASCAR, marked by seven titles and a winning percentage of 11.24 in an era when winning was more challenging than ever before. For many, it was too much, and they either backed away from the sport or refused a new hero.

Dale Earnhardt defined stock car racing for more than two decades with his aggressive driving style, no-nonsense attitude, and, eventually, the unmistakable black #3 car. A seven-time Cup Series champion, Earnhardt wasn't just a competitor – he was a cultural icon, a fan favorite, and the embodiment of NASCAR's rough-and-tumble roots.

You don't get called "The Intimidator" if you are soft on the track.

Born on April 29, 1951, in Kannapolis, North Carolina, Dale Earnhardt grew up around the sport. His father, Ralph, was a respected short-track racer, and Dale quickly followed in his footsteps. Ralph was a professional driver, and he ran where the money was, including 51 NASCAR Grand National races without a win, but he won championships in the Sportsman division.

Ralph's garage was Dale's classroom, and dirt ovals were his proving ground. By his early teens, Dale had absorbed the mechanical knowledge and old-school discipline that became his trademark. But it wasn't just about tools or cars – it was about survival. In Ralph's world, winning wasn't glamorous; it was essential.

In the late '60s and early '70s, long before anyone called him "The Intimidator," Earnhardt was scraping together parts and pocket change to race at gritty bullrings like Hickory, Concord, and Metrolina – tracks he'd known since childhood. He'd even snuck into the sport earlier. One night, with Ralph sidelined, Dale slipped into one of his dad's old cars and entered a local race under a fake name. He drove like he belonged – because he already did.

From there, it was dirt late models and stock cars, usually in hand-me-down gear, always with a chip on his shoulder. There were no big sponsors or polished crews – just borrowed trailers, busted knuckles, and a hunger to beat the guy beside him.

Those rough tracks forged the driver he became. Races weren't just about finesse; they were brawls. Contact was expected, aggression was rewarded, and respect was earned the hard way. In that environment, Earnhardt raced with elbows out and eyes forward, never backing down.

He also learned to read a car and track instinctively, developing a feel for the edge – how far he could push before the tires gave up. That fearless style made him stand out, and by the time he debuted in the Cup Series in 1975, driving a Dodge for Ed Negre in the World 600 at Charlotte, folks in the Southeast already knew the name Dale Earnhardt.

His impact wasn't immediate. It took four more years to land a regular drive after a breakout run in the 1978 World 600 at Charlotte, where he ran up front for much of the race in a car owned by broadcaster Walter Cronkite. Watching from the stands was Californian Rod Osterlund, who soon tracked Earnhardt down and signed him to lead his new team in 1979.

Seven races into the season, Earnhardt scored his first win at Bristol and earned Rookie of the Year honors after finishing seventh in points. A year later, he won his first NASCAR Winston Cup Championship with five victories. Midway through 1981, Osterlund sold the team to Jim Stacy. Four races later, Earnhardt left and joined the upstart Richard Childress Racing (RCR), then spent two seasons with Bud Moore Racing while RCR grew into what he needed.

He returned to Childress in 1984, five years after the two had traded punches

Black Goodwrench Chevrolets with the #3 on the side fitted the image of The Intimidator. This one was on display at the NASCAR Hall of Fame in Charlotte. (Alamy)

at Riverside in 1979. During that time, Childress had stepped back from driving to build a team specifically for Earnhardt.

He won his six titles for RCR in pairs. Back-to-back in 1986 and 1987, then again in 1990/1991 and 1993/1994. Despite his success, the Daytona 500 became Earnhardt's most elusive prize. He had numerous close calls and heart-wrenching defeats at the iconic track, but in 1998, after 20 attempts and with seven titles under his belt, he finally won the "Great American Race."

The celebration that followed was unforgettable: pit crews lined pit road, high-fiving Earnhardt as he rolled down the frontstretch. It was a moment of pure emotion and long-overdue triumph – one of the most iconic in NASCAR history.

Through the 1980s and '90s, Earnhardt built a reputation as one of NASCAR's fiercest and most dominant drivers. His black #3 RCR Chevrolet became a symbol of intimidation. He raced hard – sometimes too hard – but always to win.

Open face black helmet, dark goggles, and intensity all added to Dale Earnhardt's image. Here he is getting ready for the Primestar 500 at Texas Motor Speedway in March 1999. (Alamy)

That relentless style earned him the nickname "The Intimidator," replacing his early moniker "Ironhead." Fearless and calculating, with sharp racecraft and long-run smarts, he was one of the sport's most complete drivers.

Rivalries with Jeff Gordon, Rusty Wallace, Darrell Waltrip, Terry Labonte, and Bill Elliott helped elevate NASCAR's profile during a crucial era. Despite his aggressive image, Earnhardt commanded deep respect – for his skill, passion, and quiet generosity away from the spotlight.

Earnhardt wasn't just a racer; he was a savvy businessman. With his third wife, Teresa, Dale Earnhardt, Inc. (DEI) was created as a racing organization that would later field cars for his son, Dale Earnhardt Jr., and others, including Michael Waltrip and Steve Park.
But it was also a huge business with

The crash that claimed the life of Dale Earnhardt at Daytona in February 2001. (Alamy)

merchandise sales that would have made most teams dizzy.

On February 18, 2001, tragedy struck during the final lap of the Daytona 500. While blocking to protect his DEI teammates, Earnhardt crashed head-on into the turn four wall. He died instantly from a basilar skull fracture.

His death sent shockwaves through the world of motorsport and prompted sweeping changes in NASCAR safety standards – including the widespread adoption of the HANS device (a device designed to prevent the type of skull fracture that claimed his life), SAFER barriers (Steel and Foam Energy Reduction), and better car construction.

"Dale was rough," said Richard Petty. "He came up beating and banging on short tracks, doing whatever it took. He didn't mind moving someone out

Dale Junior (left) with Dale Senior in 1999. (Sporting News via Getty Images)

of the way if that's what it took to win. He only won 76 races, but the seven championships – that's what made him a legend. He wasn't polished, but fans loved that. He wasn't a cookie-cutter driver, and he didn't care what people thought. It wasn't always pretty, but it worked for him."

Earnhardt's partnership with RCR was the most rewarding on the track, and six of his titles came with that team. Childress still gets emotional to this day when you talk to him about Earnhardt, and it is rumored that somewhere inside his massive operation in Welcome, North Carolina, the wreck that claimed his star driver's life sits, untouched since the day of the crash.

"He and I raced hard back in the day – real hard," the Immortal team owner Richard Childress said recently. "I remember this one night, I won the race, and Dale finished second. He grabbed me afterwards – this was probably '76 or '77 – and he says, 'Next time I race against you, I'm gonna beat you.' We were just a couple of young, hungry kids back then, but who would've thought we'd end up sitting around having a beer years later, talking about that night … and then go on to build something so big together.

"I quit driving in '81 because I could see where the sport was headed. The big money was rolling in, and I could run in the top 10, maybe get a fifth here or there, but I didn't want to be out there just running 15th. That's when the opportunity came to put Dale in the car. He ran 10 races for me that year, and we opened a lot of eyes. I was in debt after it, but I knew we had something special.

"What made Dale great? He never wanted to go back to where he came from. He'd worked the short tracks, the trailer parks, the rough jobs – he didn't want to go back, and neither did I. That's what drove him. He had the hunger, and that's what we built the team on – raw desire. We weren't the best funded, but we had the will to win. And we had a driver who would knock the wall down to get there.

"People talk about 'The Intimidator,' and yeah, he had that look, that style. He didn't do anything wrong on track – not in my eyes. If somebody got in the way, he'd let 'em know he was faster. That black number three would show up in someone's mirror and you could see them flinch. He had that effect. But off-track? Loyal as they come. A true friend.

"He helped transform RCR. We won six Cup championships together, and between that and our Xfinity success, we've stacked up 16 or 17 titles overall. But it all really started in '81 with those

Sport needs villains as much as it needs heroes – and Dale Earnhardt was more than willing to play the villain.

10 races. He helped put us on the map. I'll never forget that.

"When we lost Dale in 2001, it changed everything – for me, for the sport, for everyone. It was like losing a brother. I wanted to walk away right then. But I remembered a conversation we had once, on a hunting trip. I'd almost died up on a mountain, and he told me, 'If something ever happens to me, you've gotta keep racing.' That's the reason I stayed. That's the reason I'm still here."

Sport needs villains as much as it needs heroes – and Dale Earnhardt was more than willing to play the villain. He wanted to race, and he wanted to win. He acted like nothing else mattered. But it did.

"Dale was one of the sharpest guys I ever met – didn't matter what kind of formal education he had," veteran team PR man Drew Brown says when recalling his time with Earnhardt. "I remember we were planning this car unveiling, and we thought we had it all sorted. Dale listened to us, shook his head, and said, 'Nah, it's gotta be more entertaining than that.' This was a guy who came from a sawmill, and here we were with all our degrees … and damned if he wasn't right. He just had that instinct – for people, for showmanship, and for what worked.

"He once told us, 'That's the problem with you sons of bitches – you ain't got no debt.' We were sitting around looking at stock prices, and he just cut straight through it. 'Debt's what motivates you,' he said. 'You need to owe something – that's what makes you get up and hustle.' It was classic Dale. Most people run from pressure – he thrived on it. That was his mindset, and honestly, that was part of what made him so great.

"And his death … that was our watershed moment. We'd lost Adam Petty, Kenny Irwin Jr., Tony Roper – not to mention serious injuries to Steve Park and others – but when Dale died, everything changed. It was like Senna in Formula 1. It wasn't just a tragedy; it was a line in the sand. From that day forward, safety became more than a discussion – it became a commitment.

"You think about it – Dale died in the first race of NASCAR's big new era, the first race on Fox, our coming-out party to the world. His car won, with a driver who'd never won before, with Michael Waltrip of all people. Shakespeare could have written the story. It was glorious and

Dale Earnhardt Sr. in his #2 Wrangler Pontiac Grand Prix while it is repaired after a wreck during the 1981 Firecracker 400 at the Daytona International Speedway, 1981. (Robert Alexander/Archive Photos/Getty Images)

devastating at the same time. NASCAR's greatest moment … and its darkest."

His impact on the sport was massive. He was its biggest name since Richard Petty, and when he died, it changed the sport.

"At that time, Dale was the guy," Richard Petty says, reflecting on the significance of Earnhardt's death. "Jeff Gordon was starting to challenge him, but he hadn't taken over yet. Then we lost Dale, my grandson Adam, and another driver all around the same time. Dale's death really brought safety to the forefront.

"They started putting in SAFER walls, changing the cars' construction – everything. Today's drivers are in a cocoon. They can barely move their heads with all the safety gear, and that's the way it should be."

Dale Earnhardt left an indelible mark on NASCAR – first as a fierce competitor and seven-time champion, and later, in death, as a catalyst for sweeping safety reforms. Racing was his escape from financial hardship and became both his passion and his obsession. He won titles, raced for nearly three decades, and earned millions – but he never knew when to stop. In the end, it was racing itself that brought his career to a close.

Jimmie Johnson was a new breed of champion, polished and professional from the minute he arrived in the sport. He changed its appeal to an audience outside NASCAR's traditional base . . . and he won seven titles. (Alamy)

Jimmie Johnson

Birth date	September 17, 1975
Place of birth	El Cajon, California
Cup Series titles	7 (2006, 2007, 2008, 2009, 2010, 2013, 2016)
Competed between	2001–present
Results	83 wins from 689 races (as of 2024)

While some drivers made headlines with fire and fury, Jimmie Johnson quietly rewrote the record books with the calm of a surgeon and the consistency of a tax return. He didn't just win – he made dominance look boring, which, in NASCAR, is the highest form of brilliance.

In a sport where thunderous engines and larger-than-life personalities have long ruled the spotlight, Jimmie Johnson built his legend differently. Quiet, composed, relentlessly focused – and unbelievably successful. With seven NASCAR Cup Series championships, 83 career wins, and an era-defining run of five straight titles, Johnson didn't just win. He reshaped what modern greatness looked like in NASCAR.

He was calm in the chaos – precision in a sport built on pressure. And as Richard Petty bluntly put it: "Jimmie was the last driver to carry NASCAR. But since then, nobody's stepped into that role. We need a face of the sport again."

Born on September 17, 1975, in El Cajon, California, Johnson was racing motorcycles by the time most kids were learning how to read. His early years in motocross and off-road trucks gave him the grit and throttle control that would later define his NASCAR style.

But he wasn't a legacy driver – he was a self-made racer who worked his way up, eventually catching the attention of Jeff Gordon and Rick Hendrick in the late '90s. That led to creating one of the sport's most iconic driver-team combinations: Johnson in the #48 Lowe's Chevrolet for Hendrick Motorsports.

His first taste of the NASCAR Busch Series – now the NASCAR O'Reilly Auto Parts Series – came at Indianapolis Raceway Park in 1998, driving for ST Motorsports. The result? A modest 25th-place finish, but the seeds were planted. He returned in 1999 with Herzog Motorsports, running a limited schedule before jumping into the deep end with a full-time campaign in 2000.

That year at Watkins Glen, Johnson endured one of the most terrifying wrecks of his young career. Midway through the race, his brakes failed entering turn one, swerving hard to avoid Dennis Demers' #86 car, Johnson shot across the grass, caught air over the gravel trap, and smashed head-on into the Styrofoam barriers at over 150 mph. It was the kind of crash that leaves spectators holding their breath.

But then came the moment that perfectly captured who Jimmie Johnson was, even before he was a champion: he climbed out, raised both fists in the air like a victor, and grinned through the pain. "I was just so happy to be alive and OK," he later said.

That moment, a wild wreck, a cool-headed response, and an iron will wasn't just a footnote. It was a preview. Before the polished trophies and seven Cup titles, Johnson showed what would come to define his career: resilience, poise under pressure, and a refusal to back down from the edge.

Between 2002 and 2005, he quickly established himself as one of NASCAR's elite. His rookie season in 2002 was remarkable – he earned the pole for the Daytona 500, won three races (including a Dover sweep), and became the first rookie to lead the point standings. Despite finishing fifth overall with 21 top 10s, he narrowly lost Rookie of the Year honors to Ryan Newman.

In 2003, Johnson continued to build momentum, winning three races and the All-Star Race, while finishing second in the championship behind Matt Kenseth. He was a weekly contender with 20 top 10s and spent 69 consecutive weeks inside the top 10 in points, the ninth-longest run of all time.

The 2004 season was emotionally charged. Johnson won a career-best eight races, including sweeps at Pocono and victories in marquee events like the Coca-Cola 600. But tragedy struck during the Chase. While Johnson was racing in the Subway 500 at Martinsville, a Hendrick Motorsports plane crashed en route to the track, claiming 10 lives – including team owner Rick Hendrick's son, brother, and key executives. Johnson, who finished second in the race, didn't learn of the crash until after the checkered flag. It was a devastating blow.

He would go on to finish second in the championship once again. In 2005, Johnson added four more wins, including his fourth straight at Lowe's Motor Speedway, known today as Charlotte Motor Speedway. He was in title contention heading into the season finale, but a crash at Homestead dashed his hopes, and he finished fifth in the standings. Over these four seasons, Johnson cemented his status as a championship-caliber driver, but not yet a champion.

Between 2006 and 2010, Jimmie Johnson did more than win – he altered the standard by which dominance in NASCAR is measured. In those five years, he claimed five consecutive Cup Series championships, something never before achieved in the sport.

Johnson kicked off the run in 2006 by winning the Daytona 500 – his first – and by the end of the season, he had clawed back from early Chase missteps to surge through with five consecutive top two finishes and take his first Cup title.

In 2007, Johnson doubled down. Ten wins. Four poles. Twenty top five finishes. He swept both Richmond races.

Jimmie Johnson during the NASCAR Winston Cup MBNA Armed Forces Family 400 in May 2003. (Jon Ferrey/Getty Images)

Both Martinsvilles. Both Atlantas. He did it with flair and a calm precision, never rattled, always calculating. By the end of the year, he had 33 career wins – already 18th on the all-time list.

By 2008, Johnson was in rare air. Only Cale Yarborough had ever won three straight titles – and Johnson matched that feat with seven wins and a career-high six poles. He swept Phoenix and delivered tactical masterpieces like his fuel-mileage win at Lowe's. For good measure, he tried his hand in the Truck Series that year – not just for fun, but to challenge himself. It was a reminder: Jimmie wasn't resting on his laurels. He was sharpening his craft.

Elliott Sadler and Jimmie Johnson lead the field at the start of the Kobalt Tools 500 NASCAR Nextel Cup series, 2007. (Alamy)

Then came 2009 – the year he made history. Johnson became the first driver in NASCAR history to win four consecutive championships. Seven wins. Sixteen top fives. Twenty-four top 10s. He won both Dover races and another at Phoenix, bringing his tally to 47 career wins and placing him firmly in the conversation with the sport's legends. Not only was he fast, but his ability to adapt across tracks, conditions, and playoff pressure was unmatched.

In 2010, he capped the streak with his fifth straight title. While others stumbled late in the Chase, Johnson executed with championship composure. Six more wins – including his first and only win on a road course at Sonoma – brought his total to 53. When the title fight tightened in Homestead, he outlasted Denny Hamlin and Kevin Harvick to seal the deal. Five in a row is a record that may never be touched.

What Johnson did between 2006 and 2010 wasn't just historic. It was transformative. He became the yardstick in NASCAR's modern playoff era. It was a run defined not by drama or brashness, but by ruthless precision and unrelenting professionalism. In a time when the sport

> He was steady, respectful, and ruthless only when the green flag dropped.

was searching for a new icon, Jimmie Johnson stepped up – and then he never stepped down.

He added title number six in 2013, and in 2016, he equaled history with his seventh after a come-from-behind win at Homestead-Miami Speedway in the season finale, tying Petty and Dale Earnhardt with seven Cup Series titles. It was the final flourish of a decade-long dynasty that had started with quiet promise and ended in roaring dominance.

Jimmie Johnson was the undisputed master of NASCAR's playoff era, especially in its formative years. He didn't just survive the playoffs – he owned them. In that five-year stretch, Johnson and crew chief Chad Knaus mastered the art of peaking at exactly the right time. While others faded under the playoff spotlight, Johnson delivered win after win, including three victories in the Chase in 2007 alone.

With 29 wins in the Chase/playoff races, he has 14 wins more than Joey Logano, who is the next best.

Even in seasons when he wasn't the dominant regular-season force, Johnson would flip the switch come Chase time. That's what made him dangerous – he could fly under the radar all year, then unleash a playoff blitz that left everyone else scrambling for scraps.

But for all the silverware, Johnson's greatness also lay in how he carried himself. He wasn't a brawler or a soundbite machine. He was steady, respectful, and ruthless only when the green flag dropped. His smooth driving style, especially on long green-flag runs, was like watching a surgeon at work – efficient, patient, and devastating when the time came to strike.

He earned the nickname "Superman" during his championship streak, not just for his speed, but for the way he shouldered expectations. He gave NASCAR something it hadn't seen before – a California cool mixed with Midwestern work ethic. He brought in new fans, especially from the West Coast, and quietly redefined what the face of the sport could look like.

After his seventh title, the wins slowed. He remained with Hendrick Motorsports through 2020 but couldn't add to his totals. No matter – his legacy was already sealed. Then, in true Johnson fashion, he took on another challenge: IndyCar. From 2021 to 2022, he tackled open-wheel racing with Chip Ganassi Racing. It wasn't about results – it was about pushing himself again, proving that even at 40-plus, he could learn, evolve, and adapt.

In 2023, he returned to NASCAR as a part-time driver and part-owner at Legacy Motor Club, shifting his influence from track to boardroom. He wasn't chasing headlines but helping build the sport's future. In 2025, he finished third at the Daytona 500, avoiding the chaos near the end to cut his way through the spinning pack.

In his Hall of Fame year, Johnson's place in the pantheon was made official. But those who worked with him already knew. Just ask Drew Brown.

"Jimmie was our ASA (a NASCAR feeder series) guy when I worked for Pennzoil," Brown said. "He was just this humble kid from a trailer park. I remember Steve Park gave him a shout-out on national TV after a win, and Jimmie never forgot it. He tells that story all the time."

And as a driver? "He's in the conversation for greatest of all time," Brown continued. "Seven titles – and he could've won 10. Before the playoff format, you had to earn it over 38 races against 40 cars. That's what makes his run even more impressive."

In 2006, Jimmie and Chandra Johnson launched the Jimmie Johnson Foundation to support children, families, and communities, with a strong focus on public education. One of its most heartfelt projects is Jimmie Johnson's Victory Lanes, a bowling alley at Kyle and Pattie Petty's Victory Junction Camp in Randleman, North Carolina, where kids with serious medical conditions can be kids.

The foundation's biggest fundraiser is its annual golf tournament in Johnson's hometown of San Diego, which has raised over $8 million for K–12 public education. Funds have been allocated to classroom technology, playgrounds, reading programs, and more, particularly in California, Oklahoma, and North Carolina – all meaningful locations for the Johnsons.

Beyond education, the foundation has supported groups such as Habitat for Humanity, Make-A-Wish, the Hendrick Marrow Program, and the American Red Cross. In 2014, Johnson also joined the Ban Bossy campaign, encouraging leadership in young girls and challenging outdated stereotypes.

In June 2020, a noose was discovered in African American driver Bubba Wallace's garage stall at Talladega Superspeedway, prompting widespread concern across the NASCAR community, albeit later shown not to have been targeting Wallace. Johnson was among the first to express his outrage. He described his initial reaction as

Jimmie Johnson in the #48 Hendrick Motorsports Lowe's Chevrolet leads a pack of cars during the NASCAR Nextel Cup Series Advance Auto Parts 500 in 2004 at Martinsville Speedway. (Robert Laberge/Getty Images)

disbelief and anger, stating, "My blood was boiling. I could not believe that had happened."

Demonstrating solidarity, Johnson collaborated with fellow driver Kevin Harvick to organize a powerful pre-race tribute. They, along with other drivers and crew members, pushed Wallace's #43 car to the front of the grid, symbolizing unity against racial injustice. This act was widely recognized as a significant moment in NASCAR's history, showcasing the sport's collective stand against racism.

The foundation and actions like this are more a measure of the man than the race driver. He wasn't the loudest guy in the garage, and he didn't stir up controversy or chase the spotlight. He just did what he needed to do, on and off the track.

He is an Immortal not because he demanded the spotlight, but because he earned it every lap, every season, every time. And off the track, he stood up for what he felt mattered.

Jeff Gordon swept into NASCAR with a new level of professionalism and presentation and claimed four titles. This title-winning celebration took place in Phoenix in 2001. (Alamy)

Jeff Gordon

Birth date	August 4, 1971
Place of birth	Vallejo, California
Cup Series titles	4 (1995, 1997, 1998, 2001)
Competed between	1992–2016
Results	93 wins from 805 races

Jeff Gordon brought an entirely new vibe to NASCAR – and with it, a whole new wave of fans who probably never would've looked twice at stock car racing. His impact on the sport was transitional and he was the first driver to win more than $150 million on his way to four titles and 93 wins.

One of the reasons for NASCAR's massive growth over the past three decades has been its ability to stretch beyond its traditional Southern stronghold. That expansion owes a great deal to the popularity of drivers like Jeff Gordon, Jimmie Johnson, Kyle Larson, and Martin Truex Jr., who weren't Southerners.

These weren't just fast drivers but cultural game-changers who broadened the sport's appeal far beyond the Piedmont backroads.

Gordon, a California native who cut his teeth in Indiana sprint cars, was the first true superstar to shatter the mold. He wasn't a product of the Southern dirt track scene. He was clean-cut, media-savvy, and resonated with fans in places where NASCAR had barely made a dent.

And that was the point – he didn't fit the mold. At a time when the sport was ruled by grizzled veterans with Southern drawls and good ol' boy swagger, along came this fresh-faced kid with a California twang, a polished media game, and a rainbow-colored race car. He didn't grow up on moonshine and red clay ovals – he came from open-wheel roots and

Jeff Gordon is interviewed on pit road before the 2006 Aaron's 499 at Talladega in full "Rainbow Warrior" gear. (Alamy)

brought a sleek, almost corporate energy NASCAR had never seen.

Gordon wasn't just a driver – he was a crossover star. He gave fans beyond the Southeast someone to get behind. People from New York, Chicago, and LA who'd never watched a lap at Talladega suddenly had a reason to care. He made the sport feel accessible to those who didn't grow up with it. Sponsors noticed. TV execs noticed. And before long, NASCAR was selling out stadiums in cities it had never dared to enter.

And he could drive, too. Gordon didn't just show up – he started winning. Quickly. He rattled cages, stacked trophies, and gave older fans a new villain to boo. That clash of cultures, that sharp divide between the traditionalists and this bold new poster boy, gave NASCAR the kind of drama that sells tickets and boosts ratings. Every hero needs a rival, and every dynasty needs a disruptor. Gordon was both, depending on who you asked.

He looked good on camera, sounded great in interviews, and knew how to work a crowd. Kids loved him. Parents bought the merch. Non-racing fans took notice. He was the total package – and he helped drag NASCAR into the mainstream spotlight, whether the sport was ready or not.

What made him special as a race driver wasn't just his impressive stats, it was the way he combined raw talent and razor-sharp racecraft with a kind of smooth, almost surgical precision that NASCAR hadn't seen before.

He came into the sport at a time when most top drivers were in their 30s and 40s, with years of short-track muscle and scars to show for it. He was 21, clean-cut, driving a rainbow-colored car, and winning almost immediately. That shouldn't have worked – but it did, because Gordon wasn't just fast, he was smart. He could read races like a poker hand. He had an innate feel for grip, strategy, and momentum, and he almost never made the same mistake twice.

What set him apart was his ability to win on any style of track and race. He mastered short tracks, superspeedways, road courses, mile-and-a-halves, and whatever else was thrown at him. He could outmuscle his rivals at Bristol, outsmart them at Sonoma, and outlast them at the World 600.

Gordon was also fearless in traffic. He could knife through the field picking off cars with moves that looked impossible from the grandstands, but made total sense when you watched the replay. He had incredible throttle control, uncanny car placement, and a sixth sense for when to attack. And when the car wasn't perfect? He still found a way to wring out results.

Then there was the mental game. Gordon didn't get rattled. He could go toe-to-toe with Dale Earnhardt on Sunday and do a national TV interview Monday without missing a beat. His poise under pressure, especially during the mid-to-late '90s when he was winning everything in sight, made it look easy.

From his colorful #24 car to his fierce rivalry with Dale Earnhardt, Gordon brought a new level of polish, professionalism, and crossover appeal to NASCAR. He helped bridge the old school with the new, and in the process, became one of the sport's most iconic figures.

Born on August 4, 1971, in Vallejo, California, Jeff Gordon was racing quarter midgets by age five. He quickly rose through the ranks of open-wheel racing, winning national championships in sprint cars and midgets as a teenager. Initially destined for IndyCar, Gordon's path changed when he signed with Hendrick Motorsports and shifted his focus to NASCAR. He made his Cup Series debut at the 1992 season finale in Atlanta – the same race that marked Richard Petty's final start. A symbolic torch was being passed without anyone knowing it at the time.

In 1993, Jeff Gordon began his first full-time NASCAR Cup Series season, driving the newly formed #24 DuPont Chevrolet for Rick Hendrick. That bright, multicolored, and instantly competitive car would soon become known as the "Rainbow Warrior."

Rainbow Warrior was at first used with a hint of mockery, especially from old-school traditionalists who saw Gordon as too polished, too clean-cut, too flashy for their rough-and-tumble world. But the nickname stuck. And as Gordon started winning it came to represent something else entirely: a new era.

Gordon won the 1993 Rookie of the Year award and claimed his first Cup win in 1994 at the Coca-Cola 600 in Charlotte. Later that year, he also won the inaugural Brickyard 400 at Indianapolis Motor Speedway.

Gordon's rise was meteoric. With crew chief Ray Evernham, he formed one of the most formidable driver-crew chief pairings in NASCAR history. Dale Earnhardt famously dubbed Jeff Gordon "Wonder Boy" in the mid-1990s, and like a lot of Earnhardt's best lines, it started as a jab but ended up becoming a kind of backhanded badge of honor.

> What made him special as a race driver wasn't just his impressive stats, it was the way he combined raw talent and razor-sharp racecraft with a kind of smooth, almost surgical precision that NASCAR hadn't seen before.

The nickname first surfaced publicly during the 1995 NASCAR season, the year Gordon cemented his place as Earnhardt's biggest threat. That year, Gordon won his first Cup title at 24 years of age, knocking off Earnhardt, who had just claimed his record-tying seventh championship the season before.

For a guy like Earnhardt, who'd clawed his way up from dirt tracks with busted knuckles and grit, this baby-faced kid with the rainbow car and the

Dale Earnhardt Jr. (#88) and Jeff Gordon (#24) battle during the Coca-Cola 600 at Charlotte Motor Speedway in 2014. (Alamy)

GORDON
24
CHEVROLET SS
MOOG
MAHLE
COMP
EARNHARDT JR
88
NATIONAL GUARD
NATIONALGUARD.com
CHEVROLET SS
MOOG
MAHLE
COMP
88

Jeff Gordon awaits the start of a NASCAR Cup race. (ISC Images & Archives via Getty Images)

corporate polish was everything he wasn't. So he gave him a nickname that sounded like it belonged in a comic book – Wonder Boy.

Earnhardt wasn't being complimentary. He was being Earnhardt: blunt, sarcastic, and protective of the old-school way of doing things. But even in the name, there was a hint of reluctant respect. Gordon was young and polished, but also fast, fearless, and infuriatingly good. And Earnhardt knew it.

Over time, Wonder Boy became part of the mythology of their rivalry. Gordon embraced it, the media ran with it, and fans picked sides. You were either with The Intimidator or the Wonder Boy, and the nicknames only helped fuel that fire.

Later in his career, as Jeff Gordon moved from wide-eyed prodigy to hardened veteran, the rivalries didn't stop – they just got more layered. No longer the young disruptor, Gordon found himself squaring off against a new generation of challengers, each bringing out a different side of his fiercely competitive nature.

Jeff Gordon at the 2015 Toyota/Save Mart at Sonoma Raceway, California. (Sarah Stierch/ Wikimedia Commons)

His battles with Tony Stewart were combustible. Stewart, the bull-headed dirt track graduate with a short fuse and a sharp tongue, mirrored some of Gordon's own earlier traits. Their clashes were often born from mutual intensity, two champions unwilling to back down. They banged doors, traded barbs, and left fans on edge every time they were near each other on the track. There was respect, but it was the kind that came with bruises.

On the other hand, Matt Kenseth was a different kind of rival. Quiet, methodical, and frustratingly calm, Kenseth's style rubbed Gordon the wrong way more than once. Things boiled over in 2006 at Chicagoland, where Gordon, fed up with Kenseth's bump-and-run tactics, hunted him down after the race and physically confronted him on pit road. It was a rare public flash of anger from Gordon, a moment that showed just how seriously he took every race and every position.

Then came Brad Keselowski, the aggressive upstart who made a habit of pushing the envelope. Their feud exploded in 2014 at Texas, when contact on a late restart cut Gordon's tire and ended his shot at the win. The aftermath saw a post-race brawl with Gordon at the center of it, bloodied but defiant. He called out Keselowski in no uncertain terms, accusing him of reckless desperation. It was a raw, unscripted reminder that Jeff Gordon was still willing to fight.

These rivalries weren't side stories but proof that Gordon never coasted, backed off, or stopped caring. Whether it was a fellow champion or a young gun with something to prove, Gordon met them all with the same intensity that had carried him to the top. Even as the sport evolved around him, the fire never went out.

Jeff Gordon's statistics speak for themselves: 93 wins, four championships, three Daytona 500 victories, five

Brickyard 400 wins, 81 poles, 797 consecutive starts, and seven Southern 500 wins. He was especially dominant on road courses, winning multiple times at Sonoma and Watkins Glen.

Though Gordon remained competitive after his fourth championship, he never won another title. However, he continued to win races nearly every year, contending regularly in the Chase for the Cup era. In 2015, Gordon announced that the season would be his last as a full-time driver. He made it memorable by winning at Martinsville, qualifying for the Championship 4 at Homestead, and finishing third in the standings in his final race.

After retiring, Gordon joined Fox Sports as a race analyst in 2016, then stepped away in 2021 to take a more active role at Hendrick Motorsports as Vice Chairman. He is a NASCAR Hall of Fame inductee, named one of NASCAR's 75 Greatest Drivers, and the man who helped reshape the sport for a modern audience.

Gordon brought an entirely new vibe to NASCAR and a whole new wave of fans. He made NASCAR accessible to people who didn't grow up in it. He rattled cages, stacked trophies, and gave older fans a new villain to boo.

As Drew Brown put it, "Jeff changed everything. He brought youth to the Cup

He rattled cages, stacked trophies, and gave older fans a new villain to boo.

Series in a way we hadn't seen. In 1996, we had a rookie, Johnny Benson, who was 31 and considered young. Jeff came in at 20 or 21. That was revolutionary.

"More than that, he helped usher sprint car drivers into NASCAR. Before that, guys came from ASA or other stock car routes. After Jeff, we saw Tony Stewart, Ryan Newman, Jason Leffler – all USAC guys – make the move. And it worked. He also took corporate sponsorships to a new level. Jeff was marketable, polished, and incredibly talented."

But he didn't just make a habit of winning races – he made a habit of giving back, too.

In 1999, at the peak of his NASCAR success, Jeff Gordon launched the Jeff Gordon Children's Foundation to support kids with serious illnesses. In 2006, he opened the Jeff Gordon Children's Hospital in North Carolina – an active, full-service facility that's helped thousands of families.

In 2007, Gordon teamed up with sporting icons like Andre Agassi and Muhammad Ali to launch Athletes for Hope, encouraging pro athletes

Jeff Gorden during qualifying for the Ford 400 NASCAR Nextel Cup race at Homestead-Miami Speedway, 2005. (Alamy)

to engage meaningfully in charity and inspiring others to do the same.

By 2011, his racing and philanthropy came together when AARP's Drive to End Hunger joined his team, targeting food insecurity near NASCAR tracks, especially for seniors.

Gordon also worked with the Clinton Global Initiative on global issues. His legacy goes beyond the track – it's about using success to drive real change.

For Gordon, legacy isn't just about trophies – it's about using your platform to make a real difference. He was the Rainbow Warrior or the Wonder Boy. And he was one of the most important figures in NASCAR history.

Shown in 1953, Lee Petty dominated when NASCAR was transitioning from a time when you could still drive your race car to the track, to an era of high-level professionalism. (Public domain: floridamemory.com)

Lee Petty

Birth date	March 14, 1914; died April 5, 2000
Place of birth	Randleman, North Carolina
Cup Series titles	3 (1954, 1958, 1959)
Competed between	1949–1964
Results	54 wins from 427 races

If his son, Richard, is known as "The King," what title should Lee Petty carry? NASCAR's first three-time champion was a force of his time, albeit a late starter to motor racing at the age of 35. He worked his way from being "dirt poor" to building an empire known as Petty Enterprises, which in various guises powered many wins for himself, his son, and his grandson.

Before Lee Petty ever strapped into a car bearing a NASCAR number, he was already carving out a reputation as a fast and fearless wheelman in the rough-and-tumble world of post-war Southern stock car racing. In this scene, moonshine, money, and motors often shared the same lane.

Born in 1914 and coming of age during the Great Depression, Petty didn't take the conventional route into racing. In fact, he was already nearing his mid-30s before he ever considered it a career path. Until then, he was a family man focused on providing for his wife and sons, working as a truck driver and even trying his hand as a biscuit salesman. But after World War II, America was changing fast – and so was the South's underground racing culture.

Like many drivers who would go on to shape NASCAR, Petty's introduction to motorsport came on dusty fairgrounds, dirt tracks, and makeshift circuits scattered across the Carolinas and Georgia. These were unsanctioned, loosely organized events that paid out cash and demanded

Lee Petty was NASCAR's first triple champion. (North Carolina State Archives/Wikimedia Commons)

bravery more than engineering. Drivers often ran without roll cages, safety gear was laughable by modern standards, and the only real rule was "don't lift unless you're upside down."

Petty didn't come from a racing family or have mechanical engineering in his background. But what he did have was natural talent, an iron will, and a farmer's toughness. He quickly figured out that he could win – and more importantly, make money – by driving hard and keeping his car in one piece. That last part set him apart.

While others were fast and reckless, Lee Petty developed a reputation for being smooth, calculating, and hard to beat over a race distance. He understood mechanical sympathy, and he knew how to bring a car home. That made him dangerous – and profitable.

By the time Bill France Sr. formalized the National Association for Stock Car Auto Racing in 1947–48, Petty was already well seasoned. He was 35 years old when he entered the very first NASCAR Strictly Stock race in 1949 at Charlotte, driving a borrowed Buick. He promptly wrecked it. But rather than fade away, he doubled down – and the rest, as they say, is legend.

That pre-NASCAR experience gave Petty an edge. While others were still adapting to longer races and bigger venues, Lee had already learned how to manage equipment, outsmart rivals, and think two steps ahead. It's no surprise that he became NASCAR's first three-time champion and a founding figure in the sport's early professionalization.

Petty's early years in Randleman were on a family farm where his parents scraped out a living. He grew up "dirt poor," meaning the family home didn't even have floorboards. With the hard times of the Great Depression in the

1930s, Petty accepted whatever jobs were available to support his young wife, the former Elizabeth Toomes, and his two sons, Richard and Maurice.

In 1943, after a freak wood stove accident, the family's house burned to the ground in front of the horrified eyes of his wife and sons.

After the devastating fire, Lee Petty and his family converted a trailer into a makeshift house. While the original family farmhouse was lost, what came next was a testament to Petty's resourcefulness and resilience. That trailer home became more than just a shelter – it was the foundation for the Petty family's rise in stock car racing.

As the family's fortunes improved with Lee's growing success in NASCAR during the late 1940s and '50s, they eventually moved into a proper home. That later house, built near Randleman, North Carolina, became the Petty family base and, in many ways, the cradle of one of NASCAR's most storied dynasties.

That later house still stands today. It's part of the broader Petty compound, which includes the original Petty Engineering shop (now part of the Petty Museum complex), and it remains a key site for fans making the pilgrimage to see where both Lee and Richard Petty's legacies took root. The modest beginnings, from trailer to triumph, are all part of the lore that shaped the "King" and his royal racing bloodline.

While others were fast and reckless, Lee Petty developed a reputation for being smooth, calculating, and hard to beat over a race distance.

In 1948, when he was already in his mid-30s, Lee entered – and won – a race in Danville, Virginia, only a stone's throw from North Carolina in a 1937 Plymouth he and his brother Julius – sometimes called Julian, Julie, or JH – had rebuilt. Interestingly, while Julius built many race cars that won many Grand National and Convertible races, he never built one for Lee or Richard in those classes, preferring to run others.

Petty came in second in his next race at Roanoke, Virginia. From the very beginning, he possessed the remarkable consistency that would be a hallmark of his racing career, finishing in the top five in more than half the races he entered.

Petty's success was due as much to his temperament as to his ability on the track. At a time when stock car racing was populated by men out for a good time, drivers who thought nothing of partying into the wee hours, before and after a race, Petty was different. Racing was

Petty's success was due as much to his temperament as to his ability on the track.

much more than merely a hobby for him, and he approached it with seriousness, calculation, and a singular determination to win, which is how his son sums up his racing style.

"He was consistent, he knew that they had no sponsorship, and he lived off the money that he made on Saturday or Sunday or whenever they raced," Richard said recently. "So, he took care of his equipment.

"A lot of guys would get in and outrun him because he had a little six-cylinder Plymouth, so he just putted around. But he finished the races, and they'd lap him or get way ahead, but they'd have trouble because they'd use their cars up.

"So, he was known as Mr Consistency. If they'd run a race, he always finished it. Most of the time, by the end of the race, he was close to the front because when he retired, he'd won more races than anybody."

Petty had more than a fierce will to win. He also recognized that only the winners would be able to pay their way in 1940s racing, where expenses often ran into several thousand dollars while the winner's purse rarely totaled more than $1,000.

Petty grew up in Level Cross, North Carolina, which even to this day isn't particularly impressive, aside from the legacy left by the Petty family, and is now known as a neighborhood of Randleman. His grave is not far from the family home, marked by a modest plaque on the ground beside his wife, Elizabeth, in the Level Cross United Methodist Church cemetery. There's a small model of the 1957 Oldsmobile that secured at least 11 wins and a title attached to the top of the plaque.

A humble place to rest for a man who built something amazing from nothing. Son Richard says when he was growing up, they knew no different, they had no idea they were poor … until his dad started racing.

"Back then, there wasn't any modern stuff," Richard says. "We lived on a dirt road about a mile off the highway. No running water, no electricity. A little three-room house. So, anything we did was new to us.

"There wasn't any TV, we didn't get a newspaper and didn't have a radio. So, you just lived that life.

"Racing got us to see the rest of the world. It woke us up to the fact that there's something out there. Being 12 or 14 years old, the only thing you did was

Lee Petty powers through the north turn on the Daytona Beach and Road Course while Junior Johnson faces the wrong way. (Alamy)

go to church on Sunday and go to school on Monday. That's the only place you go. You didn't go on vacation. You didn't go to the beach or to the mountains or any of that kind of stuff. You just lived a very simple life.

"If we were poor, we didn't know because the guys next door had the same thing we did. So, we didn't even know there was indoor plumbing or that you could turn the water on, or have electricity. Didn't have a clue about that kind of crap.

"My dad grew up in the Depression. He was born in 1914, and I was born in 1937. The big deal is that there was nothing going on. But after the war, all the people who lived our lives, the guys who had gone overseas, they'd seen other things, and they came back, and they wanted excitement again.

"Things started really progressing, especially in the South. Racing was a natural deal because everything was a little rural. Everybody had to have a car to go anywhere, and everybody thought they had the fastest car.

"So, they got to challenging each other. Bootleggers did, and then other people did. So, Bill France decided

Reproduction of Lee Petty's 1959 Oldsmobile 88 hardtop at the Richard Petty Museum in Randleman, North Carolina. (Alamy)

that some racing was happening, but it wasn't organized. France got with a bunch of other people running races and had them make an organization. Now, that's when NASCAR was born, basically in 1948. I guess they started racing. They might have run a little in 1948, but 1949 is when the stock cars started."

And that is when Lee hit the track in a car – a 1948 Buick – borrowed from his neighbor. It wasn't a race-prepped machine or part of any professional effort. It was just a regular passenger car, yanked from the driveway, barely modified, and hurled into history … but that was the point of Strictly Stock, and it suited him.

This was June 19, 1949, the inaugural NASCAR Strictly Stock event at Charlotte Fairgrounds, but the race didn't go his way. He lost control and rolled the car, completely destroying it in the process. No cage. No proper seat belts. Just raw determination and whatever steel the factory happened to weld together.

The car was a write-off, and needless to say, that neighbor probably wasn't thrilled. But Petty's mindset was clear: "If I could've won one race, and then made enough to buy me a car, I'd be ahead." That was his gamble. He wrecked the Buick – but won something far more valuable: experience, determination, and a hunger to do it again, this time on his own terms.

Within weeks, he was back on the grid in a Plymouth he owned outright. And by the end of 1949, Lee Petty had finished second in NASCAR's points standings. A year later, he founded Petty Engineering – and by 1954, he was a champion.

His 54 wins stood as the most wins until exceeded by his son, Richard, who pushed on to 200 wins, but he's a whole other chapter in this book.

For some who knew him, Lee Petty was uncommunicative, tight-fisted, and a dirty competitor. Others, however, found that he was also a gentleman.

> Two years later, he nearly lost his life in a qualifying race at Daytona.

He wasn't fan-friendly like his son would become, but he was popular nonetheless.

"Racing got my dad out of the moonshine business," his son Richard said of the early years. "He figured it was safer on the racetrack than it was running up and down the road at night with a load of liquor.

"It started in 1949, and my dad ran the very first race. I think it was $1,500 or $1,000 to win the race. He borrowed a car for the first race and returned it banged up and couldn't even pay for the repairs.

"Then he'd bought a car for $1,000, and because they were Strictly Stock, we didn't have to spend a lot of money on the car. So, we went to race a bit. I think my dad was probably the first professional racer who stopped working anywhere else and just concentrated on racing.

"A lot of the guys had cars, and then the guys who drove them just showed up on the weekends. So, it was three or four years before anybody got really serious besides my dad."

He won his first race in the first NASCAR season at Heidelberg Raceway

Petty suffered a crushed chest, punctured lung, fractured collarbone, and a broken leg, among other injuries. After days in a coma, Petty managed to pull through.

in Pennsylvania and finished that championship in second. He won a single race in each of the next two seasons, then won three races in 1952, and five in 1953. But it was 1954 that finally returned the ultimate reward from a seven-win season and his first title.

It took him another three seasons to win another title, and he followed that up immediately with a third in 1959.

Two years later, he nearly lost his life in a qualifying race at Daytona. While attempting to avoid another driver who had gone into a spin, Petty and Johnny Beauchamp hit each other. His car flew 150 feet over a wall and into a parking lot. Richard Petty witnessed the crash and described the aftermath in his autobiography: "There wasn't anything left of either car. There was blood everywhere, and they had just taken Daddy out of the car and were putting him in the back of an ambulance. He was lifeless."

Petty suffered a crushed chest, punctured lung, fractured collarbone, and a broken leg, among other injuries. After days in a coma, he managed to pull through. He spent the next four months in a hospital bed.

According to *Sports Illustrated*'s Mark Bechtel, Petty explained the accident by saying, "It was a left turn, and we went straight." However, he was never the same afterwards. His son Richard noticed the difference the next time Lee drove.

"It sure wasn't the Lee Petty of old," Richard wrote in his autobiography. "He didn't charge into the turns and he wasn't smooth. That's the part I noticed most." Petty drove in six more races, but his winning days were behind him, admitting in 1989 to the *Sporting News*'s Richard Sowers "That wreck in '61 took the desire out of me." His last win came in 1960 in Jacksonville, Florida. He hung on until 1964, then retired after a race in Watkins Glen, New York, telling his sons it was not fun anymore.

Lee Petty always supported the racing ambitions of his son Richard, who began his career while Lee was still active. When the two drove against each other, Richard experienced firsthand what a hard-nosed competitor his father was. In one of Richard's very first races, Lee took his son into the wall to pass him.

This crash at Daytona nearly claimed Lee Petty's life and effectively ended his career. Here, Johnny Beauchamp in #73 is riding over the top of the already half-destroyed #42 on its way to the car park. (Fanbuzz.com)

Richard thought he had recorded his first victory at a race in 1960 – until a protest was filed claiming that Richard was actually a lap short at the finish. The protest, made by Lee Petty, was upheld, and Lee was named the victor.

"I would have protested even if it was my mother," Lee Petty said, according to Joseph Slano of the *New York Times*. That race turned out to be his last win.

He wanted to win, but his biggest goal was to be able to win enough races to lift his family with him. And he did that. Petty Enterprises was the benchmark of the sport, and for many years, he was still active with the team that took his son past all his records.

He remained humble and grounded by his faith, hence the plaque in the ground rather than a monument to a staggering life and career. Lee Petty didn't just survive stock car racing's outlaw years – he mastered them. And when NASCAR came calling, he was more than ready.

David Pearson drove for Cotton Owens from 1962 through 1967. Together, they entered 170 races, took 27 victories, and won the 1966 Cup title. (ISC Images & Archives via Getty Images)

6

David Pearson

Birth date	December 22, 1934; died November 12, 2018
Place of birth	Spartanburg, South Carolina
Cup Series titles	3 (1966, 1968, 1969)
Competed between	1960–1986
Results	105 wins from 574 races

David Pearson won races at a rate no other NASCAR driver in history can match. He had an overwhelming sense of cool, too, and a voting panel of his peers declared him the NASCAR Driver of the Century in a *Sports Illustrated* poll.

Few names in NASCAR history command the same level of respect as David Pearson. Known as "The Silver Fox" for his smooth, strategic, and often cunning driving style and prematurely graying hair, Pearson's career is one marked by sheer talent, remarkable consistency, and understated dominance. With 105 Cup Series wins and three championships, he remains one of the sport's most iconic figures – not just for what he won, but how he raced.

Like many of the sport's greats, he had a strategic mind, and his driving style was rooted in understanding and patience. Unlike many of his contemporaries, who charged hard from the drop of the green flag, Pearson often chose to linger just behind the leaders, conserving his car, studying the field, and waiting for the perfect moment to strike.

He understood that races weren't won in the first hundred laps, and he built a reputation for being at his most dangerous when the finish line was near.

Pearson didn't just race – he orchestrated. Where others muscled cars through corners and chased grip with white knuckles, Pearson glided. In a sport full of brawlers, he was the sniper; calm in the noise, striking with a blade-sharp certainty.

Driving Fords for Holman-Moody, David Pearson was nearly unbeatable in 1968. (ISC Images & Archives via Getty Images)

That smooth, unhurried style wasn't just aesthetic – it was devastating. Pearson could coax speed out of a car without ever punishing it. His tire wear was minimal. His engines lasted. Over 500-mile marathons, he looked like the guy on a Sunday drive ... right up until the final 20 laps, when he'd drop the hammer and take the race from you before you even realized he was coming.

Under pressure? That's where Pearson thrived. He didn't just handle heat – he seemed to slow the world down when everyone else panicked. When the field got tight and elbows came out, Pearson didn't flinch. He found gaps no one else saw, timed passes to the inch, and always knew exactly how much was left in the car – and in you.

His duels with Richard Petty weren't just classics because of the stakes or the spectacle. They were chess matches. Petty raced hard, but Pearson raced smart. He let others make the first move, then dismantled them with timing and execution. He didn't need to lead every lap – just the last one. And often, that's exactly what he did.

The stats say 105 wins, but the numbers miss the nuance. Pearson didn't race with flair. He raced with intent. Quiet. Calculated. Clinical. In the heat of battle, when chaos reigned, Pearson didn't just survive – he dictated.

And that's why, decades later, drivers still speak his name with a mixture of reverence and resignation. Because they know: you could beat anyone on the right day … but beating Pearson meant being perfect.

"Pearson could run dirt, asphalt, short track, superspeedway, road courses," said team owner Everett "Cotton" Owens. "He could run anything he set his mind to. I'd say he's one of the greatest. In terms of percentage of race wins, for the races he ran, I'd say he's the greatest of all time.

"He was awful hard to get excited about anything. I'd say he was one of the coolest guys, as far as driving a race car, that I've been around."

Born on December 22, 1934, in Spartanburg, South Carolina, David Pearson grew up in the heart of stock car country and there are stories of him, as a young lad, sitting on the top of the trees he climbed outside the Piedmont Interstate Fairgrounds dreaming of the day he would run on that dirt track.

He spent time watching every nuance of the races, and that is perhaps where his innate knowledge of his craft developed. Many great racing drivers, in whatever category, can tell you their influences as drivers, how they would take the hand movements of driver X, the aggression of driver Y, and the patience of driver Z.

That smooth, unhurried style wasn't just aesthetic – it was lethal.

Pearson's influence was all of that. He believed when he was sitting in those trees, that he would be better than all of them. That he would be better than any driver, ever.

He thought he would be the greatest, and if that made him cocky, so be it.

His racing journey began on the dirt tracks of the Carolinas, which was not an unusual path. He quickly gained a reputation for his natural ability behind the wheel. He won the 1959 Late Model Championship at Greenville-Pickens Speedway, less than 50 miles from his hometown.

He made his Grand National debut in 1960 and claimed the Rookie of the Year title. In 22 starts that season, he finished in the top five three times. Pearson's early years saw him team up with influential car owners like Ray Fox and Cotton Owens. He scored his first win in 1961 at the prestigious World 600 in Charlotte (driving for John Masoni), showcasing the race craft that defined his career. He ran over some debris and punctured his right rear tire two laps from home while leading by three laps. He limped around the track, more often than not on the grass, but still managed to beat "Fireball" Roberts home.

His reputation grew quickly – not as a brash or flashy driver, but as a calculated, methodical one who knew how to win without overdriving.

He bounced between teams, lacking the continuity to really dig in. In 1962, he made 12 starts for four different teams – hardly ideal in a sport that ran 52 races that season. Things improved slightly in 1963 with 41 starts from two teams, the bulk of them with Cotton Owens, who would become a pivotal figure in Pearson's rise.

By 1964, the pieces started clicking. Pearson ran 61 of the season's 62 races – every possible event, with only one Daytona 500 qualifier available – and picked up eight wins. He had rhythm. He had consistency. And with Owens behind him, he had a car capable of staying in the fight.

But then came 1965 – and with it, politics. NASCAR banned the Chrysler Hemi engine, the same powerplant that gave Dodge drivers like Pearson and Petty their bite. Both scaled back dramatically in protest. Pearson's momentum hit pause. But only briefly.

Pearson came back swinging in 1966 with the Hemi allowed back – albeit with restrictions designed to keep Ford happy. He ran 42 of 49 races, won 15 of them, and claimed his first NASCAR title with Owens. It was a statement year, a warning shot to anyone who thought the break had dulled his edge.

Midway through 1967, Pearson made a bold move. He left Owens and joined Holman-Moody, Ford's factory-backed powerhouse. What followed were two of the most dominant seasons in NASCAR history.

He was nearly unbeatable in 1968. He wheeled the #17 Ford Torino to 16 wins from 36 top 10 finishes in 48 starts, and grabbed 18 poles. It wasn't just the volume – it was the execution. Pearson controlled races, managed tires with finesse, and made decisions with split-second clarity. On intermediates and superspeedways, he was a ghost – disappearing out front while the rest of the field scrambled behind.

The next season, 1969, was more of the same. Eleven wins. Forty-four top 10s and another title. He started scaling back the next season, and while he was winning races he wasn't racing enough to win titles.

He was lethal at the big venues – Daytona, Charlotte, Atlanta – where speed met strategy and only the most complete drivers thrived. And even when he didn't win, he was there, lurking, keeping the pressure on. Always in the mix. Always in control.

David Pearson at Riverside in 1970, where he failed to finish. He led this race for 39 of 194 laps, but did manage to win on the famous road course three times. (Alamy)

He was 36 when he started stepping back from racing with three titles and a reputation for brilliance. But, he'd proven it all – speed, skill, smarts – and done it on his terms. For a decade, David Pearson had been the gold standard. And unlike many, he knew when to ease off the throttle.

At Talladega in 1969 – the first time NASCAR raced there – he perhaps hinted at what was to come. He was one of 11 drivers to boycott the race over concerns with the tires surviving the extreme speeds of the fastest superspeedway in the series. Today, top speed at Talladega (and Daytona) is limited by using a restrictor plate, but that wasn't the case back then, and the tires were struggling.

He didn't need to run that race, so he didn't.

These two seasons were the perfect showcase of what made Pearson special: precision, patience, and the uncanny ability to make winning look effortless. While other drivers burned out chasing trophies, Pearson made it look like just another day at the office. His back-to-back dominance in '68 and '69 remains one of the most impressive stretches in NASCAR history.

No discussion of David Pearson's career is complete without mentioning

David Pearson before a race at Daytona International Speedway in 1974. (Lane Stewart/Sports Illustrated via Getty Images)

his legendary rivalry with Richard Petty. What made their rivalry special was how evenly matched they were. In the 63 races where they finished 1–2, Pearson came out ahead 33 times.

Their most famous duel came at the 1976 Daytona 500, a race that ended in dramatic fashion. The two tangled and crashed in the infield grass on the final lap. While Petty's car was unable to continue, Pearson managed to nurse his wrecked vehicle across the line for the win in one of the most iconic moments in NASCAR history.

"I probably ran more races against Pearson than anybody," Petty told me in 2025. "We ran first and second 60-something times. But where Pearson was so good was that he was steady. He was good on the road course, short track, dirt track, and superspeedway. It didn't make any difference.

"Of everyone I raced against, he was the one who never had to push to be great. It just came to him – pure, natural talent. Maybe only Tim Flock was in the same league when it came to raw ability. The rest of us had to grind for every inch. He just made it look easy."

From 1972 to 1979, Pearson drove part-time for the Wood Brothers Racing Team, an incredibly fruitful partnership. Despite not competing in full seasons by choice, he was a dominant force, especially on superspeedways. In 1973, he entered just 18 races and won 11 of them.

Pearson's time with the Wood Brothers epitomized his approach to racing: compete when the car is right, execute flawlessly, and win often. His success on a limited schedule was virtually unprecedented and remains unmatched. He was confident in his abilities and wanted to focus on quality over quantity.

The Wood Brothers typically didn't run a full schedule back then, often focusing

> While Petty's car was unable to continue, Pearson managed to nurse his wrecked vehicle across the line for the win in one of the most iconic moments in NASCAR history.

on the bigger, more prestigious races like Daytona, Darlington, and Charlotte and that suited Pearson's meticulous and calculated driving style and his desire to spend more time at home.

He was a laid-back guy from South Carolina who wasn't consumed by fame or stats. He preferred being home with his family and wasn't interested in grinding out a full calendar just to win another title. Despite racing in fewer events, he made a massive impact, winning 43 races with the Wood Brothers in 143 starts, an incredible success rate.

Pearson continued to race part-time into the 1980s, picking up his final Cup Series victory in 1980 at Darlington Raceway – a track where he remains the all-time win leader. He stepped away from the sport gradually, with his final NASCAR Cup start coming in 1986.

He was inducted into the NASCAR Hall of Fame in 2011, as part of its second class, a fitting recognition of a career that shaped the sport. He's also a member of the International Motorsports Hall of Fame and the Motorsports Hall of Fame of America.

Pearson's legacy goes far beyond statistics. He was admired for his calm demeanor, his sportsmanship, and his masterful understanding of race dynamics. Many fellow drivers considered him the most naturally talented racer they had ever seen – a man who rarely made mistakes and never missed an opportunity to win.

David Pearson passed away on November 12, 2018 at the age of 83. The outpouring of respect from across the motorsport world spoke volumes about his impact. NASCAR Chairman Jim France called him "one of the greatest drivers in NASCAR history," while Richard Petty said, "He was the best driver I ever raced against."

In an era filled with legends, David Pearson stood out not because he chased every race, but because he didn't have to. He let his results speak, and they still do.

Cale Yarborough holds up the winner's trophy after winning the 1981 Firecracker 400 at Daytona International Speedway. (Robert Alexander/Getty Images)

Cale Yarborough

Birth date	March 27, 1939; died December 31, 2023
Place of birth	Timmonsville, South Carolina
Cup Series titles	3 (1976, 1977, 1978)
Competed between	1957–1988
Results	83 wins from 560 races

Motorsport is often about the equipment and people with which you race, and Cale Yarborough is proof of that. He was great before he linked up with Junior Johnson & Associates, but after that, he was Immortal with three titles in a row.

Cale Yarborough's legacy isn't just about championships – it's about the long, grinding road he took to earn them. He didn't burst onto the NASCAR scene; he built his career slowly and relentlessly. Over 31 seasons and 500 races, Yarborough fought his way to the top, becoming one of the most significant figures in the sport's history.

He wasn't a shooting star. He was a slow burn. And once he caught fire, he was untouchable.

Cale Yarborough debuted in 1957, but it took eight years and 81 starts before he reached victory lane. That 1965 win came as NASCAR transitioned from Strictly Stock to purpose-built race cars. Even then, his rise was gradual. He finished runner-up in the championship twice before finally clinching the title in 1976, nearly 20 years after his first start. No driver has waited longer for a NASCAR championship.

Everything changed when Yarborough joined Junior Johnson's powerhouse team in 1974. The chemistry clicked instantly. Over the next six seasons, he won 47 races in 184 starts and became the first driver to claim three straight championships – a feat only Jimmie Johnson has matched.

Yarborough always had the talent and fire. But the right car, team, and

Cale Yarborough (#21) and Bobby Isaac (#71) at the 1969 Daytona 500. (Alamy)

timing turned raw speed into greatness and made Yarborough a NASCAR legend.

He was an adventurous rogue with stories about wrestling alligators, riding bulls, jumping out of planes, diving into swamps from towering cypress trees, and catching water moccasins in those same murky waters with his bare hands. He tried to show a bear who was boss and found out it was the bear. He was struck by lightning and flew and landed an airplane without ever having been at the controls of one before.

Sports Illustrated, in the weeks after he clinched his third title, described him as "5' 7" tall, but his 185-pound body gives him the bearing of a big man. He has bulky shoulders that extend into short arms with biceps the size of melons and forearms like clubs, a barrel chest and a thick, tough midsection.

"He has a round, rosy face resting peacefully atop a tree-stump neck, thinning blond hair, a broad, genuine grin and, when things are not going the way he would like them to, a grimace that so completely scrunches his face it looks like a partly deflated beach ball. Viewed head-on, Yarborough sort of resembles the Oldsmobile he races: squat and powerful, his cheeks matching the shape of the car's bulging fenders, his sunglasses the dark-tinted racing windshield."

As you can imagine from the time frames, his path to the top was not easy. On his death in 2023, Greg Engle in *Forbes* magazine said he was the last of the blue-collar drivers to be successful in NASCAR, with the sport changing dramatically after his ascension. He was a hard charger who helped put NASCAR on the TV map.

The 1979 Daytona 500 was the first live coverage of the complete race after CBS secured the rights to the race. Blizzards gripped the eastern and northeastern United States, and the near record levels of snow left a large portion of the U.S. stuck indoors with little more than a TV set for entertainment, and that helped the live broadcast of The Great American Race.

And Yarborough turned it on. It was not that he was performing for the millions; this was just him in action.

After the white flag was waved, Yarborough ran second to Donnie Allison, the brother of fellow Immortal Bobby. Down the back straight heading into turn three, he made his move. But Allison was determined to hold the low

Cale Yarborough at Daytona in 1968. (Eric Schweikardt/Sports Illustrated via Getty Images)

line into the last two turns, and that pushed Yarborough, who had played the draft perfectly, into the mud. His big #11 Oldsmobile flicked sideways, and both cars speared into the wall, allowing Richard Petty through for a win.

What happened in the moments after the checkered flag made headlines and announced NASCAR as a TV sport. Bobby Allison slowed past the wreck to check that his brother was OK, offering him a lift back to the pits.

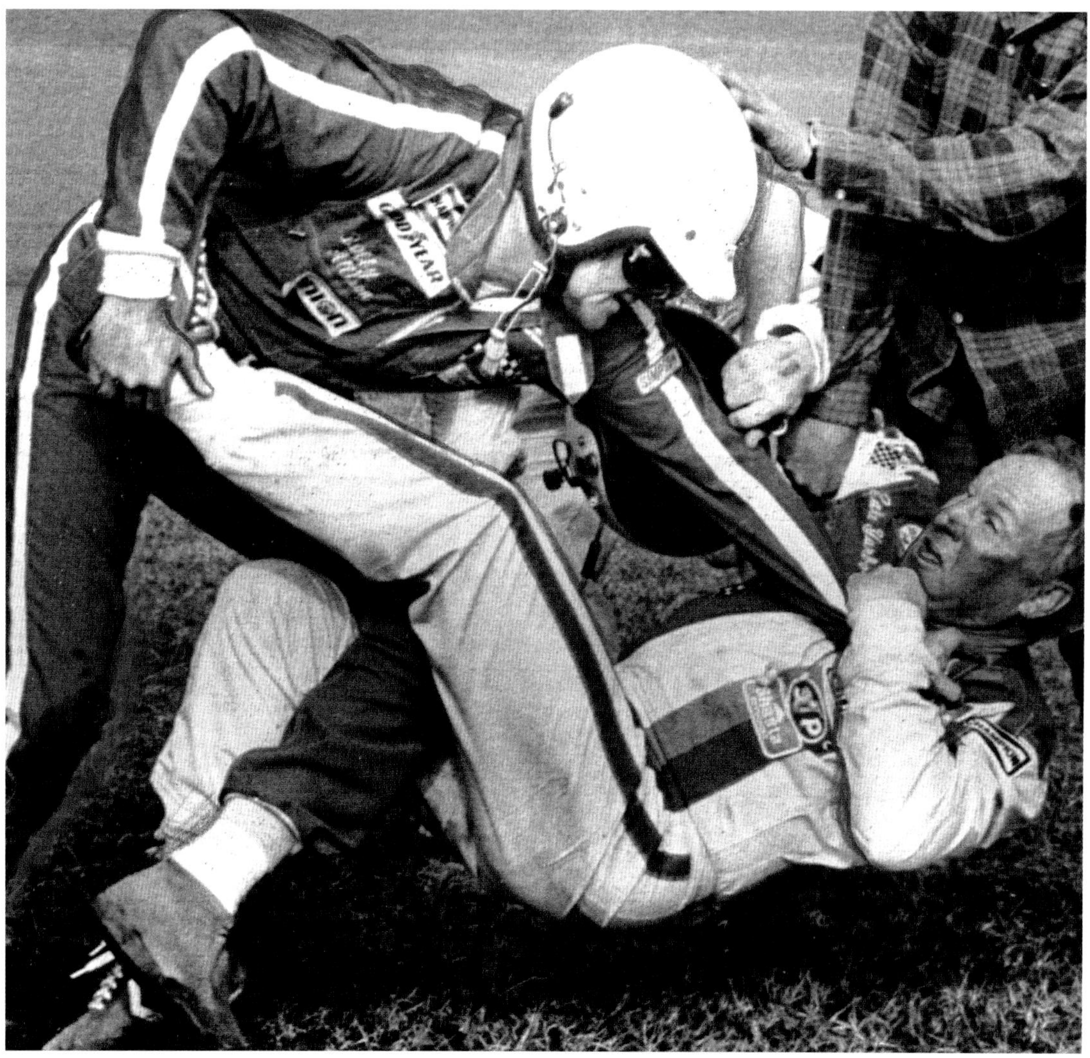

Bobby Allison has Cale Yarborough heading the ground in the fight that took NASCAR onto the front pages of the newspapers at the 1979 Daytona 500. (Alamy)

But there was more to Yarborough than just a street brawler.

Then Yarborough started yelling at his championship rival from the previous season, before swinging his helmet into his face, and fists, feet, and whatever started flying.

As with most sports, a fight made the news, and this was the first step of NASCAR moving out of the Piedmont and across the nation. But there was more to Yarborough than just a street brawler.

Yarborough was born in 1939 in Sardis, South Carolina, a tiny unincorporated village near Florence and Darlington. He said it was so small it didn't even have a crossroad. His father was a tobacco farmer and store owner who died in a plane crash when Yarborough was only 11.

A naturally talented athlete, he was a welterweight Golden Gloves boxer and a state champion during his high school years at Timmonsville, South Carolina. He was also a fullback in football and was paid to play for the Sumter Generals. Deep down, he knew from the day his father took him to the speedway each Thursday (likely in Columbia), Friday (Florence) and Saturday (Sumter), and then sat with him to listen to the Southern 500 from Darlington on the radio, that car racing would be his enduring sporting passion.

His first race car was a 1935 Ford that he paid $10 for and then built himself to run on the dirt ovals of South Carolina. He finished third in his first race in Sumter, but as he always told the story with a laugh, only three cars finished. Football and boxing were officially parked that day.

As an 18-year-old, he tried to enter the Southern 500 at Darlington after mailing a fake birth certificate and paying his $5 fee to NASCAR to get a license. When NASCAR worked out his age, he was disqualified since the starting age was 21. Later, he swapped cars with someone and made his debut, much to the angst of NASCAR, which would eventually embrace his rogue spirit.

He learned to race on the short tracks of the Carolinas, quickly earning a reputation as a fearless gun for hire. Team owners like J.N. Wilson gave the teenage Yarborough his first break, and his aggressive style soon piled up local wins – and caught the attention of Grand National teams.

Between 1957 and 1961, Yarborough ran just one Grand National race per year, starting at Darlington for Bob Weatherly, then Charlotte and

Cale Yarborough races during the Firecracker 400 at the Daytona International Speedway, 1968. (ISC Archives/CQ-Roll Call Group via Getty Images)

Daytona. In 1962, he ran four races for Julian Buesink and four more for other teams, with a best result of 10th in a Daytona qualifier.

His breakthrough came in 1965, running 45 races across seven teams and scoring his first victory at the now-defunct Thunderbowl Speedway in Valdosta, Georgia. Yarborough was a paid racer, bouncing between teams but building momentum.

From 1968 to 1970, he ran part-time with Wood Brothers Racing, claiming 11 wins. But it wasn't until 1973 that he found stability with Howard & Egerton Racing, running his first full season and finishing second in points the following year. He won 10 races in 43 starts with the team before switching to Junior Johnson's outfit mid-1974. That move changed everything – and marked the beginning of his championship run.

In the 15 remaining races of that season, he won four times to make it 10 for the season, and he finished the year second in the championship for the second year in a row.

His first full season with Johnson wasn't so rewarding, with only two wins across 30 races, but in 1976, it all unlocked with nine wins and a host of top 10 finishes, and he battled Richard Petty for the title. Fourth place in The Dixie 500 at Atlanta in the season's penultimate race was enough to secure the title as he carried an unbeatable lead into the final race at Ontario Speedway in Los Angeles.

The next season, he won the championship again with Petty runner-up, and it was even more definitive and sealed with three races remaining. In 30 races, he only missed the top 10 three times, and if NASCAR had a podium, he was there 19 times. He made it three titles in a row with another dominant season in 1978, with 10 race wins. This time, he beat Bobby Allison, with Petty going winless for the year.

"Cale and I were close. He ran for Junior Johnson and was a hell of a charger," Childress said. "I spun him out once at Metrolina on the last lap. He wasn't happy, but we got over it. He raced hard, lived fast – like Curtis Turner, one of my heroes."

The rest of Yarborough's life story veered between stock car accomplishment and surreal folklore, with varying degrees of truth behind it, that underscored his toughness.

Through it all, his roguish nature and cheeky sense of fun pervaded. Winning is not enough for immortality, although being the first of only two drivers to win three in a row is a significant marker; the way he won and the personality he brought to the sport made him special.

His huge smile and laugh when telling his stories, like flying and landing a plane for the first time because he wouldn't admit he hadn't done it before, are what made him such a popular driver.

"Cale raced for money," Richard Petty said of his great rival. "He'd win a race and jump out and say, 'How much money did I make?'"

"He was tough on equipment because he felt like he had to run as hard as he could every lap. No strategy. Except what Junior (Johnson), as crew chief, would tell him to do.

"He was one of the top two or three hardest chargers we ever ran against, one of the toughest drivers out there physically and mentally. If he was 10 laps behind, he was still trying to get to the front. He'd never give up, no matter if he had three or four wheels, it didn't make any difference to him.

"Back then, equipment was so much of what the driver could do, and

Cale Yarborough in 1981. (Robert Alexander/ Archive Photos/Getty Images)

"Cale raced for money," Richard Petty said of his great rival. "He'd win a race and jump out and say, 'How much money did I make?'"

it took him a while to get in winning equipment. Because he'd take a car that was a 10th-place car and wound up with 6th or 7th because of his driving ability, when he got in a car that was a top three or four car, he could race for the win, and he did.

"Nobody can do anything on their own. A lot of this stuff, whether a politician, football player, or racer, requires people around you to support what you can do. They allow you to shine, but they need to put you in that position. It takes a combination of efforts.

"He didn't think much about strategy – he just pushed every lap. That made him one of the toughest competitors I ever faced."

A NASCAR statement on Yarborough's death in 2023 set the legend in place: "Yarborough was a four-time Daytona 500 winner and a five-time victor in the Southern 500 – figures that rank second all time for each crown-jewel event. His three Cup Series titles came consecutively from 1976–78; only Jimmie

Cale Yarborough ran one race for Hylton Motorsports in 1972, finishing fifth at Michigan International Speedway. (ISC Archives/CQ-Roll Call Group via Getty Images)

Johnson, who won five straight crowns from 2006–10, has claimed more titles in a row. Yarborough and Johnson are tied for sixth on the Cup Series' all-time list with 83 victories each.

"The rest of Yarborough's life story veered between stock car accomplishment and surreal folklore, with varying degrees of truth behind it, that underscored his toughness.

"Yarborough is forever linked with the historic Darlington Raceway, the hard-edged track one county over where he made his big-league debut. Darlington honored Yarborough in 2016 by dedicating the same garage that he snuck into as a youth in his name. He was inducted into the NASCAR Hall of Fame in 2012 as part of the stock car shrine's third class of honorees."

"Racing is kind of like a big, tall ladder," Yarborough said during his NASCAR Hall of Fame induction speech. "When you begin, you start off on the bottom step of that ladder, and it's a long, hard climb to the top. But I feel like tonight that I'm finally standing on the top step."

Darrell Waltrip's impact on the sport went from the track to the commentary booth. (ISC Images & Archives via Getty Images)

8

DARRELL WALTRIP

Birth date	February 5, 1947
Place of birth	Owensboro, Kentucky
Cup Series titles	3 (1981, 1982, 1985)
Competed between	1972–2000
Results	84 wins from 809 races

"Boogity, boogity, boogity – let's go racin', boys!" Darrell Waltrip's famous catchphrase for the start of a NASCAR race. But before his work in the commentary box immortalized him, he was one of the greats on the track, he was a polished performer who took the off-track to a new level.

Darrell Waltrip wasn't just a champion on the track – he was a showman, a strategist, and later, the voice of NASCAR for millions of fans. With 84 career wins, three Cup Series championships, and a personality that lit up television screens, Waltrip played a pivotal role in NASCAR's evolution from a regional sport into a national spectacle.

When he first burst onto the scene in the 1970s, he was fast, sharp-tongued, and unapologetically confident. He talked a big game and, often, backed it up. That attitude earned him the nickname "Jaws," as veterans like Richard Petty and Bobby Allison weren't thrilled about the young upstart stealing the spotlight – and occasionally stealing the win. But Waltrip didn't care. He knew how to win, and he knew how to get attention doing it.

On the track, he was a master of precision and patience. Short tracks were his playground, especially at Bristol, where he won a record 12 times, including seven straight during a dominant stretch in the early 1980s. Waltrip wasn't just a driver – he was a strategist. He understood how to save

But what he lacked in humility, he made up for in talent and determination.

tires, stretch fuel, and work with his crew chief, Jeff Hammond, like a conductor leading a symphony. Their chemistry turned into championships – three in all – and helped define an era when NASCAR transitioned from a regional curiosity to a national sport.

From feuding with legends like Richard Petty to calling races from the broadcast booth, Waltrip's influence is as enduring as his signature catchphrase: "Boogity, boogity, boogity – let's go racin', boys!" which even found its way into the *Cars* movie.

Born on February 5, 1947 in Owensboro, Kentucky, Darrell Waltrip was racing go-karts and dirt track cars by his teenage years. His passion for racing matched his competitive spirit and quick wit – traits that would define his career. He made his NASCAR Cup Series debut in 1972 at Talladega. In those early years, Waltrip was considered brash and confident, not always welcome in the tradition-steeped world of stock car racing. But what he lacked in humility, he made up for in talent and determination.

Waltrip's first Cup Series victory came in 1975 at Nashville Speedway. By the late 1970s, he was winning frequently and establishing himself as a consistent front-runner. He drove for DiGard Racing early on, but it was his partnership with Junior Johnson, beginning in 1981, that elevated his career to a championship level. During the 1980s, Waltrip was arguably NASCAR's biggest star – a driver with skill, swagger, and a knack for stirring up headlines.

He made 809 starts between 1972 and 2000 during his extraordinary NASCAR Cup Series career. He scored 84 career victories – a number that places him among the sport's all-time greats – along with 390 top 10 finishes and 59 pole positions. His consistency and longevity made him a force across three decades, adapting to changes in cars, competition, and race formats.

Waltrip's prime years came during the 1980s, particularly with Junior Johnson's powerhouse team. He won three Cup Series championships, dominating with a combination of tactical brilliance, mechanical sympathy, and raw speed.

Waltrip won back-to-back Cup Series championships in 1981 and 1982, driving the iconic #11 Buick and Chevrolet. He won 12 races in 1981 and added another 12 in 1982, dominating the field with a mix of speed, patience, and tactical brilliance. He captured his third title in 1985, capping off a remarkable run that included regular

Darrell Waltrip started third and finished third in the 1985 Daytona 500. (ISC Archives/CQ-Roll Call Group via Getty Images)

wins at challenging tracks like Bristol, Martinsville, and Richmond.

Waltrip's driving style was methodical and calculated. He wasn't always the fastest off the truck, but he knew how to manage a race and be in the right place when it counted. That approach earned him 84 Cup Series wins – tied for fourth all time. Throughout his career, Waltrip was known as a polarizing figure. Fans either loved him or loved to boo him.

As the 1990s progressed, Waltrip's results began to taper off as the sport became more competitive and his focus shifted toward team ownership and eventual retirement. Still, his final decade in the sport included emotional highlights, including his long-awaited 1989 Daytona 500 win with Hendrick Motorsports. Despite going winless after 1992, Waltrip's impact never faded.

In total, Waltrip led over 23,000 laps in Cup Series competition – a testament to his front-running pace and strategic acumen. His record speaks of a driver who not only competed at the highest level for nearly 30 years but also left an enduring legacy that shaped NASCAR's evolution into a national phenomenon.

He engaged in high-profile rivalries with legends like Richard Petty, Cale Yarborough, Bobby Allison, and

Darrell Waltrip (#11) battles with Dick Brooks (#1) during the running of the 1985 Daytona 500 at Daytona International Speedway. (Robert Alexander/Getty Images)

Dale Earnhardt. His sharp tongue and confident attitude rubbed some the wrong way, but also drew attention to the sport, something NASCAR needed as it grew in the 1980s. Over time, however, Waltrip matured into a respected veteran and fan favorite. His transformation from Jaws to wise elder statesman was as remarkable as his on-track career.

For all his accomplishments, one race eluded Waltrip for much of his career: the Daytona 500. After 17 tries, he finally won "The Great American Race" in 1989, driving for Hendrick Motorsports. It was a hugely emotional victory for Waltrip, who famously celebrated with a joyful "I won the Daytona 500! I won the Daytona 500!" and he danced in victory lane with a joyous energy that showed

just how much the moment meant. It was the culmination of years of perseverance – and a fan-favorite underdog moment for a man who had once been the sport's most polarizing figure.

That win was one of his final career highlights, as his time as a top-tier driver began to wind down in the 1990s. Waltrip's later years saw him drive for his own team, Darrell Waltrip Motorsports, with limited success. He eventually joined Dale Earnhardt, Inc. (DEI) and later Haas-Carter Motorsports, but persistent struggles and changing times led him to retire from full-time racing in 2000.

Despite the tough final stretch, Waltrip's contributions to the sport were undeniable – and his transition to the broadcast booth was beginning. In 2001, Waltrip joined Fox Sports as a lead NASCAR analyst, helping usher in the modern era of NASCAR broadcasting. His passion for the sport, combined with his humor and insight, made him an instant hit with viewers.

His trademark call – "Boogity, boogity, boogity, let's go racin', boys!" – became one of the most recognizable phrases in NASCAR culture. He was a "color commentator" until his retirement from broadcasting in 2019, capping off nearly five decades in the spotlight.

Waltrip was already a star when Earnhardt arrived in the late 1970s. Polished, media-savvy, and sharp with both his wit and his wheel. Earnhardt, by contrast, was raw, relentless, and feared nothing. Where Waltrip played chess, Earnhardt often played demolition derby. Their battles began in earnest in the early 1980s, as both drivers fought for supremacy in a sport rapidly gaining popularity.

One of their most famous early confrontations came at the 1984 Talladega 500, where they traded the lead multiple times at nearly 200 mph,

"Boogity, boogity, boogity, let's go racin', boys!"

slicing through the pack in a duel that was both respectful and ruthless. Waltrip eventually won the race, but Earnhardt had made it clear – he wasn't going to back down from anyone.

Tempers boiled over a year later at Richmond in 1986, in a race that ended with both of them wrecked and angry. Waltrip had dominated much of the day before Earnhardt tapped him while battling for the lead late in the race. Waltrip spun, and chaos erupted behind them. Earnhardt won.

Waltrip didn't mince words afterwards, calling Earnhardt's move dirty. Earnhardt, ever the intimidator, shrugged it off as just hard racing. That Richmond race lit the fuse for a rivalry that only grew hotter. Both men were fighting not just for trophies but for the future of NASCAR. Waltrip represented the calculated, articulate driver who could win and then sell the sport in front of a camera. Earnhardt was the brawler who connected with working-class fans because he was one of them.

They clashed again in the 1987 All-Star Race – then known as the Winston – at Charlotte. Waltrip was leading in the closing laps, with Earnhardt stalking him in second. When Waltrip moved to block, Earnhardt pulled the infamous "pass in the grass" – a breathtaking save and power move that helped him win the race and left Waltrip furious. Though Earnhardt didn't pass him in the grass per se, he managed to keep control after sliding through the infield, muscling his way back onto the asphalt, and taking the win.

Yet for all their fiery moments, there was also respect.

As the years went on, both mellowed. Waltrip transitioned into team ownership and eventually broadcasting, while Earnhardt became the face of the sport in the '90s. They joked about their past run-ins in later years, with Waltrip often playing the showman and Earnhardt offering that sly grin, as if to say, "Yeah, I might've roughed you up a bit."

Their rivalry helped shape NASCAR during one of its most competitive decades. It wasn't just two great drivers fighting for space on the racetrack – it was two philosophies of racing colliding in every corner. And every fan had to pick a side.

Somehow, Waltrip ended up driving for Dale Earnhardt, Inc. for 13 races in 1988.

Darrell Waltrip on pit road before the start of the 1997 Daytona 500. (Alamy)

Auto.
BOSCH
Spark Plugs
Western
Auto
PARTS AMERICA
MCI
CLEVITE

Darrell Waltrip prepares for the Winston 500 NASCAR Cup race at Alabama International Motor Speedway in 1985. (ISC Images & Archives via Getty Images)

"Darrell brought life to our team when we desperately needed it," said Drew Brown, reflecting on Waltrip's stint at DEI. "We were a first-year team and had lost our driver early in the season to injury. Darrell came in and gave us stability. We started making races, even led laps. I think we ran in the top five at Pocono (he finished sixth) and California. That gave our young crew confidence. Guys like Chad Knaus and Bono Manion were just getting started, and Darrell helped elevate everyone."

More than just results, Brown remembers the human side of Waltrip: "Darrell had this amazing sense of humor. We all clicked with him – Stevie, his wife, would always be around, too. You spend so much time crammed into haulers and team rooms – you've got to get along. With Darrell, we did. And he was smart, too. Back then, drivers *were* our telemetry. He understood what made cars go fast, and he could explain it in a way that connected with everyone, from crew to CEOs. That's why he thrived as a broadcaster later."

While his driving resume was impressive – 84 Cup wins and three titles – Waltrip's influence extended beyond the driver's seat. He became one of NASCAR's most recognizable voices, both literally and figuratively. After retiring, he transitioned into a long-running career in television commentary with Fox, where his signature race-start call became part of NASCAR's identity.

He brought humor, insight, and heart to the broadcast booth, helping guide the sport through the modern TV era.

Darrell Waltrip wasn't just a champion – he was a character, a competitor, and a communicator. He drove with brains and bravado, helped build NASCAR's media presence, and left an impact that goes far beyond stats. His story is that of a racer who evolved alongside the sport, and in many ways, helped shape what it became.

In a 2012 interview, Waltrip recalled one of the most emotional days of his life, February 18, 2001, and a day the Daytona 500 ended in triumph and tragedy. "It's 11 years ago, and even today, I see that and I think about that moment in time, I could shed tears. It was tragic.

"One moment I'm excited for my brother (Michael won his first race). I'm going to Victory Circle with my brother. And the next minute I turn around and a friend of mine, Andy, was standing at the top of the steps with tears down his face. Big man, deputy sheriff in Daytona. And he's shaking his head. I say, 'I'm going to Victory Circle.' He's going to take me. 'What's wrong?' He's shaking his head and crying. He said 'We got to go to the hospital.' He said, 'I don't think Dale made it.' It was the biggest and most emotional roller coaster I had been on in my life."

That moment reminded everyone of the sport's deeper bonds. For all the rivalries and racing, the NASCAR garage was a family, and Darrell Waltrip, with all his highs and heartbreaks, was one of its most unforgettable voices. He knew how to articulate the highs and lows of the sport, and he knew how to win.

Tony Stewart was a polarizing figure in NASCAR, but the love him or hate him vibe elevated him to immortality . . . along with three titles. (Doug Benc/Getty Images)

9

Tony Stewart

Birth date	May 20, 1971
Place of birth	Colombus, Indiana
Cup Series titles	3 (2002, 2005, 2011)
Competed between	1999–2016
Results	49 wins from 618 races

Tony Stewart was something else. They called him "Smoke" for a reason – fiery on track, blunt off it, and fast in almost anything with wheels. He didn't race to play nice – he raced to win. He is perhaps NASCAR's most unapologetic outlaw.

Few drivers in NASCAR history blended raw talent, versatility, and passion quite like Tony Stewart. Known to fans and foes alike as "Smoke," Stewart wasn't just a winner, he was a racer in the purest sense of the word. Whether it was a stock car, sprint car, midget, or even an IndyCar, Stewart had one goal: beat everyone.

He is the only driver to have won an IndyCar Championship and a NASCAR Cup Series. He also has a pile of wins in drag racing, winning top fuel races as recently as 2025, proving his versatility. While he didn't win the Indy 500, he did start the 1996 race from pole after qualifying second when his teammate, Scott Brayton, who was the pole sitter, was killed in the lead-up to the race.

But it is NASCAR where his light shone the brightest.

Originally, the nickname Smoke came from his dirt track days, where he had a reputation for blistering fast laps and, more literally, for smoking the rear tires as he powered through corners. But once he jumped to NASCAR, Smoke was more about his fiery temper and what came from his mouth.

Born on May 20, 1971, in Columbus, Indiana, Stewart was racing go-karts by the age of seven. He blazed a trail through the grassroots of American motorsport, collecting titles in USAC, sprint cars, midgets, and then the IndyCar Series. His versatility was unmatched, and he didn't care what he was driving; he just wanted to win.

Over 18 full-time seasons in the NASCAR Cup Series, Stewart participated in 618 races, achieving 49 wins, 187 top five finishes, and 308 top 10s … along with three titles. He also secured 15 poles, led more than 12,800 laps, and earned over $122 million in prize money, without considering the countless millions from endorsements, sponsorships, and his post-racing business empire. Despite the chaos he could unleash on a microphone or behind the wheel, his career stats illustrate the profile of a laser-focused driver when it mattered most.

His NASCAR Cup Series debut in 1999 with Joe Gibbs Racing didn't come with a learning curve; it came with a warning to the field. Piloting the #20 Home Depot Pontiac, Stewart won three races, finished fourth in points, and walked away with Rookie of the Year honors.

In 2000, he won six races and dropped to sixth in the title. In 2001, he was the series runner-up with three wins. But it all led to the rollercoaster 2002 season, one of chaos, controversy, bruises, and ultimately triumph.

It couldn't have started worse. His Daytona 500 lasted two laps before a blown engine sent him to an early exit. But in typical Stewart fashion, he bounced back with wins at Atlanta and Richmond. By the season's midpoint, though, he was only seventh in the standings, consistent, but not yet championship-caliber.

Things took a nasty turn at Darlington, where Stewart was caught in a vicious crash and T-boned by Jimmy Spencer. He was taken to the hospital but returned the next week to Bristol. He didn't go the distance, however, and Todd Bodine stepped in mid-race. But Stewart made it clear: he wouldn't let a few broken ribs keep him off the track.

Then came the infamous Brickyard blow-up where he had a physical altercation with a photographer. NASCAR came down hard – $50,000 fine, 25-point penalty. That could've been the beginning of the end for his title run. Instead, it lit a fire. The next week, he went out and won at Watkins Glen. The win itself wasn't without controversy – he jumped the final restart, but officials let it stand. It was a classic Smoke moment: messy, emotional, and ruthlessly effective.

That win sparked a critical run of form. While he didn't win again that year, Stewart reeled off top 10 finishes like

Tony Stewart runs the highline on A.J. Allmendinger in 2016 at Charlotte Motor Speedway. (Zach Catanzareti Photo/Wikimedia Commons)

clockwork, staying consistent while his rivals stumbled. He took the points lead at Talladega and held his nerve through the final race. At the end of the year, he edged out Mark Martin to secure his first NASCAR Cup Series title, then known as the Winston Cup.

It was a fittingly chaotic path to the top. Injuries, controversy, penalties and none of it derailed him. If anything, it fed the fire. The 2002 season didn't just prove Tony Stewart could win a championship – it showed he could take everything that was thrown at him and still come out on top. It was also his final year driving a Pontiac, closing the book on a chapter that ended, fittingly, with confetti.

Tony Stewart's 2003 and 2004 campaigns didn't reach the heights of his 2002 championship, but they were defined by steady consistency and flashes of brilliance. In 2003, he had two wins and a string of strong finishes, ending the season seventh in points. The next year, he was just as dependable – two more wins, a sixth-place finish overall. He wasn't the headline act, but he was always a threat: sharp, scrappy, and never far from the action. It was the calm before the next storm.

His 2005 season wasn't just a return to form; it was a career-defining masterclass that proved he wasn't just one of NASCAR's most talented drivers but also one of its most complete. At 34, in what many consider his prime, Stewart traded some of the volatility that marked his earlier seasons for calculated aggression and championship poise, and the result was his second NASCAR Cup Series title.

The year started strong, but it truly caught fire in the summer stretch. Stewart ripped off five wins in high-profile, high-pressure races: Sonoma, Daytona, New Hampshire, Indianapolis, and Watkins Glen. The win

Tony Stewart (#14) and Dale Earnhardt Jr. (#88) spin across the finish line while wrecking during the mid-season NASCAR race at Daytona in 2014. (Alamy)

Joe Nemechek (#01), Ricky Rudd (#21), and Tony Stewart (#20) in the 2005 Budweiser Shootout at Daytona. (Harold Hinson/Sporting News via Getty Images)

at the Brickyard was deeply personal; Stewart had said for years he'd give up a championship to kiss the bricks at his home track. In 2005, he didn't have to choose. That win also handed him the #1 seed going into the Chase for the Cup, and he made it count.

In classic Stewart fashion, his victories came with a bit of flair – after each win, he climbed the fence. Fans loved it. Sponsors loved it even more. Home Depot cashed in with cheeky promotions like "Hey Tony, we've got ladders," and even ran a brick discount after his

It was a classic Smoke moment: messy, emotional, and ruthlessly effective.

Brickyard triumph. He was a marketing machine, complete with fence-climbing grit and small-town humor.

That season he won a staggering $13.5 million, including over $6 million for clinching the title, a record-setting haul at the time.

Reflecting on the season, Stewart said he appreciated the 2005 title even more than his first. It was a more composed, mature run – still fiery, still ferociously competitive, but with the kind of discipline that defined the best. It was a championship earned not by surviving the chaos, but by mastering it.

Then came the boldest move of his career. In 2009, Stewart left the safety and success of Joe Gibbs Racing (JGR) to become a co-owner and driver at Stewart-Haas Racing. Plenty thought it was a vanity project, but he proved them wrong, immediately. That season, he won four races and made the playoffs, becoming the first driver-owner to win a Cup race since Ricky Rudd in 1998.

Two years later, Stewart produced one of the greatest playoff performances in NASCAR history. After limping into the 2011 Chase with a winless regular season, he erupted, winning five of the 10 playoff races, a feat that has only been matched by Kyle Larson but never beaten.

At the 2011 season finale in Homestead, Tony Stewart went head-to-head with Carl Edwards in a winner-take-all battle. Stewart passed more than 100 cars throughout the race on his way to victory lane and the championship on a tiebreaker. It was his third Cup title, his first as an owner-driver, and the last time anyone has done it, as owning and running a competitive NASCAR team has only become more complex and costly in the years since.

Not every superstar played the game like Jeff Gordon. Where Gordon was polished and PR-trained, Stewart was flammable and unpredictable, more maverick than media darling. That's exactly why he became such a lightning rod within the sport. He wasn't universally disliked, but he was absolutely polarizing. Fans either wore his merch or wanted to see him in the wall. Inside the garage, the feelings were much the same.

He didn't care who you were – driver, official, journalist, sponsor – you knew where you stood with Smoke. He called out NASCAR regularly, once sarcastically suggesting wins be awarded based on post-race interviews instead of results. He mocked the system, clashed with officials, and kept sponsors on their toes. Stewart was pure sandpaper in

Tony Stewart before the Chevy Rock & Roll 400 at Richmond International Raceway in September 2006. (Nigel Kinrade/Sports Illustrated via Getty Images)

Tony Stewart during practice for The Winston on May 16, 2003 at Charlotte Motor Speedway, North Carolina. (Rusty Jarrett/Getty Images)

a world of corporate polish and squeaky-clean PR. That made him a nightmare for marketers but a dream for fans craving authenticity.

And on track? He was just as combustible. Stewart wasn't above dumping a driver he felt had wronged him, throwing a helmet, or having a long memory about who'd blocked him X races ago. The rivalries were real. The grudges lasted. But so did the respect.

Because underneath all the fireworks was a generational talent. Stewart could do what few others could: jump from discipline to discipline, series to series, and still run up front. He made it look effortless from IndyCar to NASCAR, from dirt to Daytona. He didn't care about optics; he cared about performance.

Stewart never forgot his dirt-track roots even at the height of his NASCAR career. He continued to run sprint and late model races, owned Eldora Speedway

– where he helped bring NASCAR back to dirt with the Truck Series – and advocated tirelessly for the survival of grassroots racing.

After suffering a broken leg in a sprint car crash in 2013, Stewart began scaling back. He retired from full-time NASCAR competition after the 2016 season – but not before delivering a final, emphatic reminder of who he was. That year, he won at Sonoma with a daring move in the final laps, outdueling Denny Hamlin in his 49th and final Cup win.

However, perhaps the toughest time of his motor racing career unfolded on August 9, 2014, during a sprint car race at Canandaigua Motorsports Park in New York. Midway through the event, Stewart and Kevin Ward Jr. touched, sending Ward's car into the wall. Ward exited his vehicle and walked down the racetrack under yellow conditions as the caution flag came out. Stewart's car struck Ward with the right rear tire, fatally injuring the 20-year-old.

The incident sent shockwaves through the motorsport world. Stewart withdrew from the NASCAR Cup Series race at Watkins Glen the following day. He later gave a tearful statement upon returning to competition, calling it "one of the toughest tragedies I've ever had to deal with, both professionally and personally." A grand jury declined to file criminal charges, and it was revealed that Ward had high levels of cannabis in his system, which prosecutors said may have impaired his judgment. The emotional toll on Stewart was clear and lasting.

Regardless of, and perhaps because of, the controversies, he remains one of the most divisive yet revered figures in NASCAR history. You either loved him or hated him, and he was fine with that.

His former PR rep, Drew Brown, was with him that season.

"He was fantastic to work with. Funny, intense, but fair. You always knew where you stood with him, and he was consistent, which made my job easier."

In retirement, Stewart has remained just as active and just as influential. Under his leadership, Stewart-Haas Racing blossomed into one of NASCAR's elite teams, winning the 2014 title with Kevin Harvick and remaining a consistent playoff threat until its shutdown in 2024.

Tony Stewart's legacy isn't just etched in stats or trophies. It's written in fire and dirt. He raced with his heart on his sleeve, spoke his mind with no filter, and treated every lap like it was his last. He wasn't here to be liked; he was here to win. And in a sport that often leans too far into polish, that kind of raw honesty mattered.

Joey Logano during qualifying for the Xfinity 500 in 2025 at Martinsville Speedway, Virginia. (Jeff Robinson/Icon Sportswire via Getty Images)

10

Joey Logano

Birth date	May 24, 1990
Place of birth	Middletown, Connecticut
CupSeriestitle	3 (2018, 2022, 2024)
Competed between	2008–present
Results	32 wins from 541 races (as of the end of the 2024 season)

They called him "Sliced Bread" before he even baked a Cup win – and for a while, it looked like the hype might stale. But Joey Logano proved he wasn't just fresh talent – he was the whole damn bakery, serving up championships with a side of swagger.

Joey Logano has carved out a remarkable career in NASCAR, one defined by resilience, evolution, and an unrelenting drive to compete at the highest level. Born on May 24, 1990, in Middletown, Connecticut, Logano showed promise early on, making headlines in the racing world as a teenager and eventually becoming one of NASCAR's top-tier drivers. Today, his career is far from over, and he remains a formidable force on the track.

Joey Logano's path to NASCAR stardom began before most kids had a learner's permit. By age seven, he was already winning championships; by 10, he'd conquered bandoleros, legends, and late models. Recognizing his rare talent, his family moved to Georgia to chase the racing dream, where he caught the eye of Randy LaJoie, who dubbed him "Sliced Bread," as in the best thing since sliced bread, and Mark Martin, who famously predicted Logano could become one of NASCAR's all-time greats.

Logano didn't just arrive in NASCAR – he was launched into it with the kind of hype that usually ends in headlines or heartbreak. At just 18, he was tapped to replace Tony Stewart in the iconic #20 Joe Gibbs Racing Toyota, and the expectations

Joey Logano leads the pack in the 2025 Daytona 500. (Alamy)

were sky-high before he'd even turned a lap.

His Cup debut was scheduled for Richmond in 2008, driving the Home Depot-backed car, but it never happened. Rain and Tropical Storm Hanna washed out qualifying, and without owner points to fall back on, Logano didn't make the grid. A few weeks later, he finally got his shot at New Hampshire, making history as the first Cup driver born in the 1990s to start a race.

The following year, 2009, began with a bang – or more accurately, a crunch. Logano became the youngest driver ever to qualify for the Daytona 500 … and promptly crashed out, finishing dead last in a baptism by fire.

But he bounced back fast. By April, he cracked the top 10 at Talladega. Then, in June at Loudon, the rain came, the strategy played out, and history was made. At 19 years and 35 days, Logano became the youngest Cup

Series winner ever, breaking Kyle Busch's record. He didn't just win; he survived, adapted, and proved he belonged. The victory earned him 2009 Rookie of the Year honors and confirmed what the insiders already suspected: the kid wasn't just hype.

The following seasons were a mixed bag. In 2010, he showed promise: a pole at Bristol, seven top fives, and 16 top 10s. But he lacked the firepower to break into the elite tier, finishing 16th in points. In 2011, things regressed. Just four top fives, six top 10s, and a forgettable 24th in the standings – a season that, in hindsight, marked the beginning of the end of his tenure at Joe Gibbs Racing (JGR).

Behind the scenes, change was brewing. Longtime crew chief Greg Zipadelli exited after 2011, replaced by Jason Ratcliff in 2012. The pairing brought flashes of speed – Logano won his second career Cup race at Pocono in convincing style, passing Mark Martin late and holding off a pack of veterans. It was his first win in a race that went the full distance, and it showed he could win on merit, not just weather.

Still, it wasn't enough. Logano finished 17th in points that year, his final season with Joe Gibbs Racing. He left with two Cup wins, some bruises from the spotlight, and a reputation still trying to catch up with the hype. But in the Nationwide Series, he bowed out strong, winning a season-best nine races in 2012, showing everyone that the talent was real. It just needed the right environment to flourish.

That environment would come next, with Team Penske.

His move to Team Penske in 2013 marked the true turning point of his Cup Series career. After being cut loose by Joe Gibbs Racing, many wondered if "Sliced Bread" was stale. But Roger Penske saw potential and gave Logano the #22 Ford with Shell/Pennzoil backing. A slow-burn rise followed, turning Logano from a promising talent into one of NASCAR's elite.

Logano's first year with Penske was imperfect, but it sent a clear message. He won his first race with the team at Michigan, made the playoffs for the first time, and finished a career-best eighth in the standings. It was a mix of fiery incidents – most memorably a bitter run-in with Denny Hamlin at Auto Club Speedway – and quiet determination. Logano wasn't just surviving anymore. He was racing like he belonged.

By 2014, the switch had flipped. Logano reeled off five wins and found himself in the thick of the inaugural playoff format, a revised version of the Chase, finishing fourth in the final standings. He was no longer the

Fuel spews out of Joey Logano's Mustang following a pitstop at World Wide Technology Raceway in Madison, Illinois, 2023. (Alamy)

underperforming prodigy; he was a contender.

The following season began with a statement win in the Daytona 500, making him the second-youngest driver to win NASCAR's biggest race. He went on to win six races that year, including a playoff stretch where he swept all three Round of 12 races. That run ended with a thud – literally – when Matt Kenseth wrecked him at Martinsville in a controversial act of revenge. The crash knocked Logano out of title contention and cemented his status as one of the sport's most polarizing figures.

The 2016 season brought redemption, albeit with more playoff heartbreak. He won three times, including in the playoffs at Phoenix, and reached the Championship 4 for the first time. But at Homestead, after a late-race crash with Carl Edwards, Logano's title hopes were undone by damage and circumstance. He finished second in the championship standings behind Jimmie Johnson.

Then came 2017 – a cold dose of reality. Logano won early in the year at Richmond, but the victory was later declared "encumbered" due to a suspension infraction. That stripped him of automatic playoff eligibility

He didn't just win; he survived, adapted, and proved he belonged.

and, with inconsistent form through the season, he ultimately missed the postseason entirely. It was a sharp fall from the Championship 4 just one year prior.

In 2018, Logano responded the only way a top-tier driver can – with a championship. While most of the spotlight was on the so-called "Big Three" of Kevin Harvick, Kyle Busch, and Martin Truex Jr., Logano quietly and methodically built one of his most complete seasons. He controversially won at Martinsville with a bump and run on Truex to lock himself into the final four and then put together a flawless performance at Homestead, passing Truex with 12 laps to go to secure his first title. After years of promise, Logano had finally delivered when it counted most.

The following seasons cemented his consistency. He won multiple races in 2019 and reached the playoffs again in 2020, making another Championship 4 appearance after a clutch win at Kansas. He finished third in the title race, continuing to prove that Penske's investment was still paying off.

In 2021, Logano won the inaugural Bristol Dirt Race and remained in playoff contention, but was knocked out in the Round of 8. Then, in 2022, he reclaimed the top spot in the sport, winning at Las Vegas to punch his ticket to the final four and then dominating the Phoenix finale to claim his second Cup Series title. He became just the second active multi-time champion behind Kyle Busch.

The 2023 season didn't go as planned. Despite a win at Atlanta, Logano was knocked out early in the playoffs after a crash at Bristol. He ended the year 12th in the standings – respectable, but far below the standard he'd set for himself.

Then came 2024. Logano grabbed the pole for the Daytona 500 – Team Penske's first – and later went on to win the NASCAR All-Star Race and survive five overtimes at Nashville for his first points-paying win of the year. In the playoffs, he struck early with a Round of 16 victory at Atlanta and fought his way into the Championship 4.

At Phoenix, he got the job done again, outdueling his teammate, reigning champion Ryan Blaney and lifting his third Cup Series Championship trophy. It wasn't without controversy – his average finish of 17.1 for the season was the worst ever for a title winner under either the Chase or playoff

Joey Logano during qualifying for the Kobalt 400 at Las Vegas Motor Speedway in 2014. (Jonathan Ferrey/Getty Images)

formats, but once again, Logano proved that winning the right race at the right time is all that matters.

Despite the stats backing his run – solid consistency, clean execution in the playoffs, and a clutch performance when it mattered, plenty of fans weren't buying it. Social media lit up with frustration, claiming the format gifted him the title, that others were faster across the year, or that Logano simply "played the system" better than he raced.

It wasn't the first time Logano wore the black hat. He's long been one of NASCAR's most divisive figures: too polished for some, too aggressive for others, and never afraid to block, bump, or blast past a rival if that's what it took. This time, the criticism came sharp and quick, fueled by playoff fatigue and the sense that the year's dominant performers got caught flat-footed at the wrong time. Again.

"He didn't dominate the season – he dominated one race," one fan wrote on X, echoing the sentiment of many. "That's not a champion, that's a loophole winner."

Whether fair or not, the backlash wasn't new territory for Logano. He's been booed on driver intros, called

Before he was a champion, Joey Logano was known as "Sliced Bread," as in the best thing since . . . (TaurusEmerald/Wikimedia Commons)

A winner at the Illinois 300 in 2022. (Alamy)

"two-faced" by fellow competitors, and has rarely been the fans' favorite. But none of that seems to bother him. If anything, he leans into it.

"Sometimes the booing just means you're doing something right," Logano said in the post-championship press conference, flashing the same grin that has irked fans for more than a decade. "I didn't make the rules – I just won under them."

And he's not wrong. NASCAR's championship format rewards the driver who delivers in the final four, not necessarily the one who was best from February to October. Logano understood that better than anyone – and made sure he was standing tall in November.

Logano's time at Team Penske has been the ultimate career revival story. From discarded talent to generational champion, he's delivered every bit of what was promised – and then some.

Joey Logano's Cup Series career spans 18 seasons from 2008 through early 2025, racking up an impressive 588 starts, 36 wins, 167 top five finishes, and 288 top 10s. He's also claimed 31 pole positions and led more than 9,150 laps over 162,000 race laps completed.

Away from the track, he's quietly built a powerful philanthropic presence through the Joey Logano Foundation, which focuses on giving second chances to children and young adults facing tough circumstances, particularly those

> "Sometimes the booing just means you're doing something right."
> *– Joey Logano*

dealing with homelessness, foster care, food insecurity, and addiction recovery.

Founded in 2013, the foundation's mission is built around the belief that "everyone deserves a second chance." It's more than just writing checks or making appearances; Logano has personally invested his time and resources into building meaningful programs and partnerships with grassroots organizations across the United States. For instance, the foundation's "JL Kids Crew" initiative gives kids from underprivileged backgrounds a chance to experience NASCAR up close, providing entertainment and inspiration.

My first interaction with Logano was at Pocono in 2019, when he flew a young lad and his family to the rural track in upstate New York. It wasn't just a token gesture, either; I had to wait while Logano sat and talked with him. You could tell by the interaction it wasn't a chore, it was a pleasure.

One of Logano's most visible contributions came in the aftermath of the COVID-19 pandemic, when his foundation – alongside Team Penske and Elevation Outreach – committed $1 million to COVID-19 relief efforts. That funding supported both medical facilities and families impacted by job loss and food shortages, with a focus on providing meals, supplies, and mental health resources.

He's also been active in disaster relief, supporting communities devastated by hurricanes and floods and working with organizations like Convoy of Hope to deliver emergency aid. Logano doesn't just lend his name to campaigns – he shows up, rolls up his sleeves, and leads from the front.

"People forget how young Joey started," says Drew Brown. "He didn't shine right away at Gibbs, and they moved on. But then he went to Penske and flourished. That's a lesson in patience. Sometimes we rush young drivers. He just needed time.

"And he's mastered the modern playoff system. The guy thinks about Phoenix all season. He's sharp."

He's a three-time champion with plenty of years to add more, and he is one of the great personalities of the sport.

Buck Baker was one of the toughest drivers NASCAR has ever seen, and he never took a backward step, either on or off the track. (ISC Images & Archives via Getty Images)

11

BUCK BAKER

Birth date	March 4, 1919; died April 14, 2002
Place of birth	Richburg, South Carolina
Cup Series titles	2 (1956, 1957)
Competed between	1949–1976
Results	46 wins from 635 races

Buck Baker came from a tiny town, a blink and you'll miss it village in South Carolina; a stubborn racer who rarely took a backward step … on or off the track. He was a natural racer, going from his first race in 1939 to back-to-back Grand National titles in the mid-1950s. He first celebrated success and wealth with the Kiekhaefer Chrysler team, and then as a factory-backed Ford driver and went from obscurity to immortality.

The first years of NASCAR were not for the faint-hearted, and just as stock car racing evolved from the no-holds-barred attitude of moonshine running, so too did NASCAR. It was a world that suited Buck Baker, and not just because he had natural talent, but because he also had that toughness.

The sort of toughness that allowed him to win a race using a wrench in place of a broken steering wheel, which, given the nature of the tracks in those days, was bordering on superhuman.

Early reports listed him as a "bus-driving orphan farm boy from Chester, SC," which was just up the road from Richburg, where he was born. "I didn't go to the racetrack to make friends," he is quoted as saying early in his career, which was true, but it was not at the exclusion of friendships or admiration.

He was the first driver to win back-to-back titles in 1956 and 1957, and he continued racing nearly 20 years later, although he was only occasionally on the track for the main NASCAR

Replica of the Dirt Modified racer that Buck Baker made his name in. (Trekphiler/Wikimedia Commons)

series from 1967 onwards. He escaped the major injuries that some of his peers suffered, and he retained his energy for and love of the sport right to the end.

In addition to life as a bus driver, he was also called a "liquor hauler," and for him, like many, the rough and tumble of a dirt oval was less threatening than racing the back tracks of the Carolinas at night without headlights while running away from law enforcement and revenue collectors.

Baker entered his first stock car race in 1939 in Greenville, South Carolina, where he also attended his first race meeting. He left the race meeting as a spectator, telling his friends that the racers weren't doing anything he couldn't, and that planted a seed, which eventually germinated before and after WWII.

He was right about being able to do what the racers were doing, and he began to develop a career, earning wins in the minor leagues as a hard racer with a fiery temper. His first race was in 1939, and he was scared to a certain degree, but also not daunted. "When I saw all those other drivers, I realized that they wanted to win that money just as much as I did," Baker recalled. "But I didn't have to worry. A tire came off my car, and I was lucky I got it off the track."

It is reported that the arguments after races would often run for longer than the race itself, which NASCAR then, as now, loved. There is talk of tire irons, wrenches, and plenty of fists. Baker was often involved.

He began his NASCAR career with the Modifieds in 1948 and then with two Strictly Stock races in 1949, scoring his first of 46 wins in 1952 and his final one in 1964. Across his two championship seasons, he won 24 races and was part of the most dominant team, run by Carl Kiekhaefer, the sport has seen from early 1956 to its end.

Baker had the occasional win during the 1940s and ran quite strongly in the 1948 Modified title, coming 10th overall. In the first year of Strictly Stock, he ran two races in the #87 Chrysler under two team owners – Penny Mullis and then Buzzy Boehmen – before entering the 1950 season with his own team. He ran nine races that year and finished second in the final round at Occoneechee Speedway.

He had run in 11 of the 27 races of the first two seasons of the top NASCAR category. In 1951, he added another 11 from the 41-race season, but still did not win a race. The following season, four races into his campaign and in the sixth race of the season, and his third race in a Hudson Hornet, the breakthrough win finally happened at Columbia Speedway, South Carolina, less than an hour's drive from his hometown.

"I didn't go to the racetrack to make friends."
– Buck Baker

Between May and June of 1952, he also ran in the 1952 NASCAR Speedway Division season for Penny Mullis and won his first major race at Darlington in a Cadillac Special. He ran all seven championship races, winning one in addition to the non-championship race for the new class at Daytona Beach. He won $5,485 and comfortably beat 1951 Modifieds champion Wally Campbell, who was killed racing a sprint car in 1954, to the championship.

The Speedway Division rarely aligned with the Grand National Series, and that winning weekend in Darlington was the last time until the end of that season that he could run in both series on the same weekend, with often more than 600 miles between race venues. From the second weekend of May, he didn't run a Grand National race until the Asheville Weaverville Speedway race in August.

His success in the Speedway Division didn't go unnoticed either. It left him with a desire for more, and he eventually joined the Griffin Motors team, which propelled him to the front

"I saw that Buck was my top competition. There is only one thing to do with a man like that – hire him."
– Carl Kiekhaefer

of the field in 1953. Across 33 races that year, he recorded four wins and 16 top five finishes, including back-to-back victories at the brutal and challenging Langhorne Speedway, Pennsylvania, and the tamer yet equally complex Columbia Speedway, in South Carolina.

Baker's 1953 season came to life with a marquee victory at the Southern 500, his first win in NASCAR's toughest endurance race at Darlington Raceway. He capped off the season in style, winning at Langhorne Speedway and finishing fourth in the championship standings – his best result yet.

He rolled that momentum straight into 1954, starting the year red-hot with four second-place finishes in the opening five races. Baker followed up with wins at Wilson and Charlotte in North Carolina, added another at Morristown in New Jersey, and conquered the Memphis-Arkansas Speedway on the Arkansas side of the Mississippi.

By the time the dust settled on the '54 season, Baker had notched four wins from 34 starts, landed 16 top five finishes, and climbed to third in the final points standings – a sign that the veteran from South Carolina was evolving into one of the era's most consistent and dangerous competitors.

The 1955 season was more grind than glory for Buck Baker, but the numbers still told a story – three wins from 42 starts and a staggering 23 top five finishes. He was relentless. But he wasn't yet dominant.

Why? Because domination belonged elsewhere. That year, 27 of the races were won by the Chryslers of Petty Enterprises and Carl Kiekhaefer – a factory-backed blitzkrieg that left the independents scrambling for scraps. But not Buck Baker. He wasn't just hanging on – he was punching back.

Running Oldsmobiles and Buicks under his own banner, Baker was one of the few who could go toe-to-toe with the might of Kiekhaefer's finely tuned war machine. And Kiekhaefer noticed.

"I saw that Buck was my top competition," he later admitted. "There is only one thing to do with a man like that – hire him."

So, Kiekhaefer picked up the phone: "If you're as big a son-of-a-bitch as everybody says you are," Kiekhaefer barked down the line, "I'm curious – would you like to drive for me?"

Buck Baker (right) with mechanic Jim Rose at a 1950s NASCAR Modified race. (ISC Images & Archives via Getty Images)

It was less a job offer and more a challenge. Buck Baker, of course, accepted. And the game was about to change.

He had one race for Kiekhaefer in the 1955 season and then joined the team from the fifth race of the 1956 championship – the first race of the 1956 calendar year – won that race and never looked back. He won $30,090 in prize money on top of a wage rumored to be at least $1,200 a month and unreported bonuses at a time when the average median family income in the USA was estimated at $4,800 a year.

Buck Baker (#301) battling fellow Immortal Herb Thomas (#92) through the south turn of the Daytona Beach and Road Course in 1956. Fonty Flock (#500-B), Frank Mundy (#300-B) were part of a six-car team entered by Carl Kiekhaefer (Owner) in a race that was won by Tim Flock (#300-A) in another of the Chryslers. (Alamy)

Talking about the rapid evolution of NASCAR, Baker said, according to *American Racing Classics*, "Mr Kiekhaefer brought us from the kitchen to the dining room."

He ran 48 of the 56 races, won 14, and claimed his first title from teammate Speedy Thompson and Herb Thomas. Thomas was leading the series when Thompson hooked bumpers with him, sending Thomas into a horrific crash, into the hospital, and out of the final three rounds of the series, two of which Baker won to win the title.

But just as Baker was winning and happy with the team, Kiekhaefer walked away from the sport, closing down his team after a spectacular two-season run in

which he won 51 of the 90 races entered, including a 16-race winning streak during Baker's championship season, of which Baker won eight.

Out on a limb and the reigning champion, he ran initially for Hugh Babb (four wins from 15 starts), and then with himself as the team owner, for six wins from 25 starts. He only finished outside the top 10 twice.

It was good enough for a second title, leading the points from Martinsville in May when race leader Billy Myers crashed with Tom Pistone, gifting the win to Baker in a shortened race. Myers ended the crash in the crowd.

The first back-to-back champion in NASCAR history started 1958 in a brand new '58 Chevy, but after problems in the first three races, he reverted to the '57 model that took him to the title. He picked up three wins and then added another six wins in the next six seasons.

Two of those wins were in the Southern 500, which gave him three wins in the race regarded as the hardest race

Buck Baker poses with his 1958 Chevrolet during the NASCAR Cup season. He was unhappy with the '58 model, and later switched back to a 1957. (ISC Images & Archives via Getty Images)

to win in NASCAR. In 1960, he won in a shower of sparks, running the final two laps with a flat tire, and added the third in 1964, which turned out to be his final win at Cup Series level, finally scaling back his racing after the 1966 season at the age of 47.

Baker's career was marked not only by his impressive longevity and competitiveness but also by his remarkable versatility as a driver. He showcased his skills in modified cars, stock cars, and open-wheel cars, achieving back-to-back premier series titles with different teams – one year in a Chrysler and the next in a Chevrolet.

Beyond his racing achievements, Baker, along with two partners,

Buck Baker with Al Wheatley's Mercury prior to the start of the Southern 500 NASCAR Cup race at Daytona International Speedway in 1952. Baker finished ninth in the race. (ISC Images & Archives via Getty Images)

promoted races by leasing racetracks such as Charlotte Speedway and Air Base Speedway in Greenville during the 1950s. Even after retiring in 1976, Baker remained deeply involved in the sport. He established driving schools in Rockingham, Bristol, Atlanta, and Darlington, where he mentored future stars like Jeff Gordon, Tony Stewart, and Ryan Newman.

"He was one of the first heroes of NASCAR – almost like a movie star," Junior Johnson said in Baker's 2013 NASCAR Hall of Fame induction video.

"He didn't seem to have to work as hard at it as a lot of other drivers to become very good," fellow Immortal Ned Jarrett said in the same video. "Just a natural born race driver."

At the induction ceremony, his son, Buddy, himself a 19-time winner in NASCAR, said: "My father was the most giving person in the world. I've watched – and Sue (his wife) was talking about it the other day – when Richard Childress was starting out, he came to the back of my dad's truck and wanted to borrow something, and he just opened the truck up and said, get what you want. He was that type of guy.

"But that same guy with 10 laps to go, he might put you out of there if you run into him. He lived by that theory. He raced you the way you raced him.

"If you come down there mad after the race, he'd stop you about six feet away, he'd say, you take one more step, I know what you're here for, and they're going to carry you back where you came from …

"All those guys, they just got out – they had fought a war, got out of the Navy, come back to no jobs, no anything, and it was a means to feed the family. And they took it to heart. Like my dad said, 'I wouldn't want my own grandmother in that corner ahead of me on the last lap'."

Joe Weatherly, seen here in 1954, was named one of NASCAR's 50 Greatest Drivers. He was killed in a racing accident at Riverside, California, in 1964. (ISC Archives/CQ-Roll Call Group via Getty Images)

Joe Weatherly

Birth date	May 29, 1922; died January 19, 1964
Place of birth	Norfolk, Virginia
Cup Series titles	2 (1962, 1963)
Competed between	1952–1964
Results	25 wins from 230 races

Joe Weatherly is unique among these Immortals because he started racing on two wheels, winning three AMA Grand National Championships before switching to stock cars and winning two Grand National Series. He is also the first of our Immortals to die racing, meaning we can only speculate where an entire career could have ended.

When Joe Weatherly was killed in a racing crash in 1964, the newspapers of the day farewelled the "Clown Prince of NASCAR." He once cut laps wearing a Peter Pan suit, rode a donkey in the occasional drivers' parade, and enjoyed many parties while on the road. He even stole all the keys from the cars on the grid once before the "Gentlemen Start Your Engines" command was given.

Standing at most 5' 6" tall – some reports have him as short as 5' 3" and hence being known as "Little Joe" – with a rounded face, button nose, and gruesome scar, he wasn't Hollywood handsome, but he made up for it with his engaging personality and ability to talk to anyone.

In the late 1950s, Joe Weatherly and fellow Ford driver Curtis Turner became legends not just for their speed, but for their wild lifestyles. With support from Ford and track promoter Paul Sawyer, it's said they rented a Daytona house during Speedweeks – stocked with food, liquor, and party supplies at $1,000 a day.

The scar on Joe Weatherly's cheek, often mythologized as the mark of a Nazi sniper, actually came from a violent car crash in his hometown of Norfolk.

Weatherly was a born entertainer – he'd drink from a vase, spin endless stories, and pull off pranks that became racing folklore. Some of their antics even inspired Hollywood: the rental car chase in *Days of Thunder* and the motel pool scene in *Cannonball Run* both trace back to Weatherly and Turner.

But behind the antics was a serious racer. Unlike many of his wild-era peers, Weatherly could go fast *and* go the distance. That consistency brought him wins, titles, and a legacy that matched his personality – larger than life, but always competitive.

His love for speed began as a pharmacy delivery rider in Norfolk, Virginia. He liked what the machine could do – and soon found himself racing. That pursuit was paused by World War II, where he served like many young Americans. But when he returned, he hit the track and started winning.

He claimed three AMA (American Motorcycle Association) Grand National Championships in single races and took back-to-back victories in the prestigious Laconia Classic in 1948 and 1949, riding for Harley-Davidson on a tough one-mile dirt-and-asphalt course. Equally skilled on road courses and dirt ovals, Weatherly's talent was clear, but so was his appetite for speed, both on and off the track. His wild reputation back home matched his results.

The scar on Joe Weatherly's cheek, often mythologized as the mark of a Nazi sniper, actually came from a violent car crash in his hometown of Norfolk. Around midnight on October 2, 1946, Weatherly misjudged a sharp S-bend at 26th and Leo Streets, clipped a gutter, and slammed into a tree.

The car carried three couples. His girlfriend at the time, soon to be his wife, Jean Flanagan, broke both legs. Another passenger, Eddie Baines, died days later. Weatherly was thrown through the windshield, slashing his cheek and neck and severing his jugular. He likely would have died if not for the quick action by nearby police officers who knew him well.

"It was speed, which is what he was known for," attending officer Charles D. Grant told *The Virginian-Pilot* in 2007. "Anybody who knew Joe Weatherly would tell you that he'd run a car as fast as he could. He was one we knew. He was bleeding profusely. He'd have died in a few more minutes."

Joe Weatherly began the 1963 season in Pontiacs until the factory program dwindled down. He and team owner Bud Moore then switched to Mercurys for the rest of the season. Weatherly finished eighth in the Daytona 500 with this car. (ISC Archives/CQ-Roll Call Group via Getty Images)

Weatherly, already driving without a license, faced a homicide charge that was later reduced when it was revealed he'd broken the steering arm on impact with the gutter. Witnesses confirmed they had stopped moments earlier to talk with a friend, suggesting he wasn't driving recklessly. He was fined $400 and given two suspended 30-day jail sentences.

He and his mother, Carrie Kellam – owner of the car – were sued by Baines's family and by Flanagan and her mother. The suits were settled through insurance, and in 1948 Weatherly married Flanagan, whose courtroom testimony about the broken steering may have spared him from harsher penalties.

The incident didn't change him, though. Instead, he got more involved in racing, and the transition from road warrior to racer was spectacular, as detailed earlier. At first, it was Harley-Davidson motorcycles, then Fords and Pontiacs in NASCAR.

In his first season in the Modified class in 1950, he won his debut race and then added another 49 wins, making it 50 from 83 races that season. He finished runner-up in the overall standings. Two seasons later, he won 49 of 83 races on his way to the Modified National Championship and then won 52 more races and a second championship the following season.

He was making lots of money and had been building cars with Paul Sawyer in the early 1950s, and when the opportunity to buy Wilson Speedway in

Joe Weatherly (#9) leads fellow Immortal Lee Petty (#42) at Daytona in 1956. (Alamy)

North Carolina arose, the pair pitched in together. They then added the Atlantic Rural Fairgrounds racetrack, which is today known as Richmond Raceway, and the Virginia Beach speedway, not far from Weatherly's hometown. Sawyer bought Weatherly out in 1956 and evolved Richmond into one of the most loved tracks on the tour, while Weatherly focused on his racing.

Weatherly ran his first race in the Grand National class at the 1952 Southern 500 at Darlington and followed with his next race two years later at Wilson Speedway. He was a professional driver, and he raced where the money was, which for him was Modifieds and then the Convertible series until it folded after the 1959 season. Still, for all his success in Convertibles, he never added a title.

With that series gone, he needed to find a way to get into the Grand National category, which had bigger pay checks than the lower series but a higher entry cost. It was nothing like it is today, but it was a leap. He ran six races in 1955, 17 in 1956 and 14 in 1957. His first win was in his 48th start at Fairgrounds Speedway in Nashville.

Then in 1960 he linked up with Holman-Moody and raced a Ford in 17 races and ran another seven races that

He careened off the track and slammed sideways into the wall with enough force for his head to come out of the window and slam into the concrete retaining wall.

season for other teams, including three in a Plymouth for Fred Wheat. He won three times in a month for Holman-Moody, and they were his only three wins for the year, which was enough to show what he could do.

But it was 1961 when it all started to come together, running a Pontiac for legendary team owner Bud Moore in his first year of operation as Bud Moore Engineering. He won the opening round of the season in November 1960 for Doc White and then started with a win for Moore in the Daytona 500, the first race of 1961. He won seven more races that season – making it nine wins from 25 starts, and finished the season in fourth place, with those in front of him running 46 (champion Ned Jarrett), 47 (Rex White) and 38 (Emanuel Zervakis) races, but between them only had one more win than Weatherly, who was the wins leader for the season.

Weatherly and Moore went into the 1962 season to win. They ran 52 of the 53 races, which was all you could run, given you could only do one of the two Duels at Daytona qualifying races. The Clown Prince of NASCAR had evolved from the fun-loving racer and title winner in the junior categories to a serious player in the Grand National Series, and he racked up the wins. By mid-season, he had the points lead and never relinquished it, claiming a comfortable title from Richard Petty.

It was a good time to be a winner in NASCAR, as factory money exploded. Chevrolet, for instance, increased its total sponsorship from $385,000 in 1956 to $2.6 million in 1957, and the three factories spent in all categories, including the Convertibles, where Weatherly was winning.

But just as they were increasing sponsorship and reaping the rewards of "win on Sunday, sell on Monday," they all bailed out when the American Manufacturers' Association banned manufacturer involvement in NASCAR, which changed the financial dynamics and made everything more fluid.

Weatherly chased teams in 1963 that would help him win a title, not individual races. He drove for nine teams in five different car brands, more than any other champion in one season in more than 75 years of racing in the top tier of NASCAR.

He won the 1963 crown, again with Petty in second, but only won three races to Petty's 14. His strategy worked. In all, six drivers won more races than him, but only two of those won more money than him, and no one collected more points. His final win for the year was a total domination, leading 127 of 167 laps after starting on the pole and winning by more than a lap at the one-mile Occoneechee Speedway.

He started the 1964 season with a second place in a Bud Moore Pontiac a week after the 1963 season finished at Riverside Raceway in Los Angeles in a Bud Moore Mercury. Then he drove a Mercury for Bill Stroppe, a Ford for Sherman Utsman and then another Ford for Ray Osborne, before going back to a Mercury for Bud Moore again … The same car in which he finished the 1963 season.

Heading to Riverside for the first time that season, he was the points leader in the championship, but his quest for a third title in a row came to a sudden and violent end. He lost control of the #8 Mercury Marauder S-55 coming into turn three of the now-defunct track. Some say he'd lost his brakes, but there is no confirmation of that fact, although Moore is quoted as saying new parts in the brake system failed, while others who witnessed the crash pointed more at transmission issues on the 86th of 185 laps.

He careened off the track and slammed sideways into the wall with enough force for his head to come out of the window and slam into the concrete retaining wall. He didn't like being restrained in the car too much, and his safety kit was minimal. He may have had a lap seat belt and that's it, but more likely, even that wasn't connected.

Because of the lack of restraints or an optional window net, a relatively innocuous crash turned fatal. The head contact with the wall killed him instantly, and several years later, NASCAR, after a similar Richard Petty crash, mandated the use of window nets.

"Joe was wild – on and off the track," Petty said. "He came from motorcycles and brought that go-for-broke style with him. He loved to have fun, always pulling pranks, carrying rubber snakes, stuff like that. But he could race."

Weatherly's death at Riverside was a turning point. "He didn't have a window net, and when he hit, his head came out of the car. When I had my bad crash at Darlington in 1970, I started using a net, too. Eventually, it became standard."

The New York Times, reporting on his death, said: "Joe Weatherly, who lost his life in a freakish accident on the Riverside (Calif.) Raceway last Sunday,

Joe Weatherly, Fireball Roberts, and Eddie Pagan pose with their cars after qualifying for the front row of the Southern 500 NASCAR Cup race at Darlington Raceway in 1958. (ISC Images & Archives via Getty Images)

was one of the nation's most popular auto-race drivers.

"This 5-foot-7-inch competitor with the mop of brown, curly hair, a scarred cheek and a sly sense of humor was a real 'goer.' He considered himself fortunate in being able to earn a living at his hobby and he raced whenever he could, though many times he had to rent or borrow cars to reach the starting line.

"Weatherly could be a clown with his 'deep South' drawl and his pranks. He could be intensely serious when talking about business. But his most impressive trait was his courage."

He is the first of two NASCAR champions to lose their life during a championship season – Alan Kulwicki being the other when he died in a plane crash – and even though he was 41 at the time, most observers felt there were many more races, wins, and titles for the popular driver. Many honors have been bestowed upon him posthumously, but his attitude to life and his skills as a racer have earned him immortality.

Herb Thomas is widely regarded as the first superstar of NASCAR. (ISC Archives/CQ-Roll Call Group via Getty Images)

13

Herb Thomas

Birth date	April 6, 1923; died August 9, 2000
Place of birth	Olivia, North Carolina
Cup Series titles	2 (1951, 1953)
Competed between	1949–1962
Results	48 wins from 228 races

Herb Thomas was NASCAR's first two-time champion, winning his titles in the Fabulous Hudson Hornet and inspiring the Doc Hudson character in the *Cars* movie. From his first win at Martinsville in 1950 through to 1956, he was a force in the sport and could easily have won four or more titles with a little more luck and the ability to run in more races. His injury-shortened career is still one of the most spectacular in NASCAR history.

The first references to Herb Thomas in the early literature of NASCAR describe a skinny tobacco farmer, but he was just the spark that NASCAR needed as its stars were aging and the sport was under attack from the nation's politicians and moralists without vision. Thomas was part of a new wave of drivers, alongside Junior Johnson, Curtis Taylor, and Fireball Roberts, who replaced drivers like Red Byron, helping to keep the sport relevant and thriving.

While promoters with small tracks understood the power of the sport, many on the fringes didn't, and by the middle of the 1950s, there was a big push to shut it down. They viewed it as dangerous, citing the 84 deaths in the crowd after a crash at the 1955 Le Mans 24-Hour Race as a prime example of what was wrong with motor racing.

But NASCAR, not even a decade old, was growing so rapidly that it, along with other motorsports in the States, could avoid the calls for its cull.

Herb Thomas (left) finished third in the Motor City 250 NASCAR Cup race at the Michigan State Fairgrounds but won the Jim O'Donnell Sportsmanship Award. (ISC Images & Archives via Getty Images)

Thomas is widely regarded as the first superstar of NASCAR. He was the first to win more than $100,000 in prize money, he won 48 races in the Grand National Series, but it didn't start with a rush and nearly didn't get there at all. He also still boasts the highest winning percentage of any driver with more than 100 starts, which, given the competitiveness of modern NASCAR, is unlikely to be threatened.

In stark contrast to Red Byron, NASCAR's first champion, Thomas was a win-or-bust driver. When he started running in Modifieds, he didn't win a single race and rarely even finished, either wrecking or blowing up his car in one way or another. He is quoted at the time as saying, "Second place is never good enough," but life may have been easier if he had finished second and bagged some prize money.

He started racing in 1946 after watching a Modified race at Greensboro, North Carolina, and the following week, the tobacco farmer who also worked in a mill, found a car and went racing, albeit with little success. He ran Race 1 of the Strictly Stock series at Charlotte in a Ford but retired with damaged springs. He didn't finish at Daytona or Occoneechee Speedway (no reason is specified) in the next two rounds. Then he missed the next few races before recording his first finish in the Wilkes 200 at North Wilkesboro Speedway in the eighth and final round. He had 132 points and was credited with 25th … hardly the sort of stats that screamed immortality.

The following season, he had 13 starts in the 19 races and scored his first win in the series at Martinsville after starting 19th of 21 cars. He led 135 laps of 200 and was the only driver to run the full distance, making the race his own after Curtis Turner, the only other driver to lead a lap that day, retired after 66 laps.

The win was just what he needed; he was running out of money and motivation as both a team owner and driver, a rare combination even back then.

"My money was running low, I was really disgusted," he said many years later. "I thought about quitting racing and going back to the sawmill business. But when I won Martinsville, I decided to hang around a little longer."

But having unlocked the winning formula and without that blockage in the way, he became a smarter racer.

Thomas started to develop a following in the sport at this stage. Like Byron before him, he was not a hard-drinking womanizer, unlike many of the drivers, which aligned him with many of the country folk of the Southern states; he was just a serious racer. He was often characterized as a "dirt poor bush hillbilly," which in many ways was true, and he saw motor racing as a way of getting a better life than that of 'baccy farmer that had to work in the local sawmill to make ends meet and keep racing.

That is why those years without winning required a great deal of self-belief. It took a lot to get onto the track … much like Lee Petty, who was a bakery truck driver and similarly grounded in racing rather than "life."

But having unlocked the winning formula and without that blockage in the way, he became a smarter racer. The win-or-bust mentality had calmed somewhat, and now he was a clever race strategist,

Thomas broke every record that existed in one season after leading the title from March and never being headed. His records include the most wins and top five finishes, the most pole positions, the most laps led, and the most prize money earned.

but more than anything, he had raw speed. Daytona Beach local Henry "Smokey" Yunick was a racer at heart who fine-tuned his mechanical skills on planes in WWII, and out of his garage.

Yunick helped team owner and driver Marshall Teague prepare his Hudson Hornets for racing, and when Hudson wanted a second car, Thomas was the driver Teague wanted. Yunick first resisted, but after Thomas ran some practice laps at Darlington, he was convinced. Thomas had an earlier run in a Hudson at Michigan State Fairgrounds, where he ran only 26 laps of 250 after the car retired with overheating issues, but the switch to the factory team was different.

"That son-of-a-bitch could flat haul ass, and you could see he was in total control," Yunick said of that Darlington run in his book, *All Right You Sons-A-Bitches.*

The combination of Thomas, Yunick, Teague, and the Fabulous Hudson Hornet was irrepressible. He won at Darlington by more than a lap – the biggest paying race of the season, with a total purse of $23,740 and $8,800 for the winner. He won again in his Plymouth two races later at Central City Speedway in Macon, Georgia, before switching to the Hudson for the remainder of the season where

Herb Thomas in the Chevrolet #92 car at the 1956 Daytona race. (Alamy)

he won four more times in the car, and his seventh and final win for the year in Jacksonville with only three races remaining was enough to claim an unbeatable lead in his first championship from the luckless Fonty Flock.

He continued to win in 1952, running in 32 of the season's 34 races, earning eight wins from 10 pole positions. Neither of the factory-backed Hudsons for Thomas and Teague ran the opening round of the season at Palm Beach Speedway, where Tim Flock won in a customer Hudson, but then they took first and second at Daytona the next week, with Teague the winner in a 61-strong field. The race was

Ray Thompson (#390) spins out as Bill Widenhouse (#68), Fireball Roberts (#22), and Herb Thomas (#92) get ready to race past him during the 1956 NASCAR Daytona Beach and Road Course race. (Alamy)

called three laps early after the tide started to come in and take away the "beach straight."

The battle between Thomas and Tim Flock was stunning in the middle of the season. Both ended the year with eight wins, the most of anyone in the championship. Thomas won three of the final four races, but Flock hung on to claim the title by 106 points, having run one extra race for the season. Thomas missed two races and could easily have won the title if he had run those two races.

Learning the lessons of 1952, he ran all 37 races of the 1953 season and claimed 12 wins and 12 pole positions to run out a comfortable winner of the NASCAR Grand National Series from Lee Petty, who won five races in the first 20 of the season. Thomas broke every record that existed in one season after leading the title from March and never being headed. His records include the most wins and top five finishes, the most pole positions, the most laps led, and the most prize money earned.

The following season brought another 12 wins for Thomas, five more than Lee Petty, who was more consistent for the year and claimed the crown. In terms of records, Thomas became the first driver to win a second Southern

500 at Darlington, which, then as now, is regarded as one of the toughest races to win.

But the Fabulous Hudson Hornet was on the wane in 1955 as the other manufacturers caught up, and this season appeared much more disjointed than those of the past. He started the season in his Hudson, then drove a Packard before a Chevrolet, another Hudson and then a Buick. He had only one win from his first 11 races, five of which had been in a Hudson.

On May 1, 1955 his season took a turn for the worse when he was thrown from his rolling car on the Charlotte dirt track and hospitalized for a few weeks with a broken leg and other internal injuries, returning to the track at the

Herb Thomas in his "Fabulous Hudson Hornet," 1952. (ISC Archives/CQ-Roll Call Group via Getty Images)

Forsyth County Fairgrounds on August 7 for a DNF in a Hudson in a race won by Lee Petty.

At Raleigh Speedway in North Carolina two weeks after his return, this time in a Buick, Thomas was back in victory lane, just as he was the following week when in a Chevrolet for the historic Southern 500 at Darlington Raceway (NASCAR's first and for many years only paved oval for the Cup Series), which is the event he targeted in his mind as he recovered in hospital.

He won the race by more than a lap, running the lightweight but underpowered Chevy to victory lane on a set of special Firestone tires that Yunick had sourced from a junkyard in Ohio. Thomas's third win at Darlington was perhaps the sweetest after all that time out of the driver's seat.

In all, he missed 22 of the season's 45 races and finished in fifth spot, which was a remarkable effort. He won three times in that season, having opened the season back in February with a win at Palm Beach Fairgrounds Speedway, Florida.

The 1956 NASCAR Grand National Series began in November 1955, and Thomas won the final race of 1955, marking the start of the new season. He finished third on the track, but first and second place were disqualified for technical violations. In all, he won five of 48 races in a 56-race season – the longest up to that point in NASCAR history – and he finished second in the series to Buck Baker, who took his first championship title.

Thomas led the series from Baker at the Cleveland County Fairgrounds in Shelby, North Carolina, on October 23, with only four races left in the season. On lap 109 of 200, Thomas passed "Speedy" Thompson – Baker's teammate – to take the lead of the race, who retaliated by running into the rear of Thomas, spinning him sideways into the outside guardrail and rolling his Chevrolet. Then Jack Smith plowed into him, sending the Chevrolet rolling again. At least eight other cars were involved in the crash.

The two-time champ suffered a fractured skull, a badly lacerated scalp, a ruptured eardrum, and internal injuries that left him in a coma. He was rushed to the hospital where he underwent brain surgery and was, by all reports, lucky to be alive.

According to an article in *Speedway Media* in 2010, Thomas is reported as saying: "I don't remember much about it. I remember passing Speedy, and the last thing I remember is going straight into the wall. That's all I remember from that night."

He retired as one of the all-time greats, and was a key inspiration for Doc Hudson in the *Cars* movie.

Which is as well given the nature of what went on. He ran only three more NASCAR races and retired as one of the all-time greats, and was a key inspiration for Doc Hudson in the *Cars* movie.

Motorsport success can be measured in statistics, and the best winning percentage in history cannot be denied. Add in the fact that he was and remains the fastest driver to reach 40 wins (151 starts) compared with Jeff Gordon, who is the next best on 186. In the six seasons before the cracked skull cut short his competitive racing, he won two titles and was second three more times.

"He was as good as they come," fellow Immortal Richard Petty told Nascar.com. "There have been very few guys who had more confidence in what he could do than Herb. He was so strong-minded that he willed his wins and what he was doing on the track."

Tim Flock was NASCAR Cup champion in both 1952 and 1955. (ISC Images & Archives via Getty Images)

Tim Flock

Birth date	May 11, 1924; died March 31, 1998
Place of birth	Fort Payne, Alabama
Cup Series titles	2 (1952, 1955)
Competed between	1949–1961
Results	39 wins from 187 races

Tim Flock has the second-best win rate in NASCAR history and is the most successful of four siblings who dominated the early years of post-World War II stock car racing. A two-time champion, he shot to fame by racing with a rhesus monkey as a co-driver … true story. But look past the novelty factor, and you'll discover a brilliant racer who claimed two Cup Series titles.

Tim Flock wasn't just a racer – he was a character straight out of motorsport folklore, a man who brought flair, finesse, and a touch of the absurd to NASCAR's gritty early years.

Born in 1924 as the youngest of 10 children, Julius Timothy Flock came from a family that didn't just dip a toe into stock car racing – it cannonballed in. The Flocks were racing's first dynasty, a wild Southern crew from Fort Payne, Alabama, who turned heads, bent rules, and set records in equal measure.

Dubbed the "Mad Flocks" by the press they were as colorful as they were competitive. And in the middle of it all was Tim, the most talented and perhaps the most outrageous of the bunch.

Tim's brothers Bob and Fonty were pioneers in the post-war bootlegger-to-big-time-racer pipeline. Bob, the eldest, was a rough-and-tumble racer while Fonty was a dashing crowd-pleaser who nearly won the 1951

Flock's mastery of the Daytona sands was near-mythical.

made history as one of NASCAR's first female competitors.

But Tim wasn't just part of the ensemble. He was the headline act.

The three brothers qualified in the top five for the first Strictly Stock race in 1949, and Fonty (second) and Tim (fifth) finished inside the top five, while Bob's car expired from the lead on the fifth lap.

According to the racers and experts of the day, Tim was the smoothest driver on the track. His natural style and mechanical sympathy suited NASCAR's heavy, brutish cars and bumpy dirt tracks to perfection. In an era where finesse often gave way to brute force, Tim had a deft touch.

He captured the Grand National Championship twice, first in 1952 and again in 1955. That '52 season was a landmark year – not only did he dominate the points race, he became the first driver to win both the Daytona Beach and Road Course event and the title in the same year.

Flock's mastery of the Daytona sands was near-mythical. He remains the only driver to win in all of NASCAR's top divisions – the Grand National (1955 and 1956), Modifieds (1956), and Convertibles (1957) – on the original course.

Statistically, his record stands tall even decades later. Tim won 39 of his 187 Grand National starts – a win rate of just over 20 percent, second only to Herb Thomas by the slimmest of margins. One more win for Flock – or one less for Thomas – and the conversation about NASCAR's winningest driver would read differently.

"Tim was one of the first drivers I really looked up to," fellow Immortal Richard Petty recalled. "He was smooth. You wouldn't notice him during the race, but at the end, he was usually the one who won. Between Tim and my dad, I learned how to race the smart way."

He started racing in 1947 and won at his second race meeting at the Greensboro Fairgrounds, where he began competing in the junior classes before joining the Modified series with his brothers in 1948. He finished third in 1948 with one win; he was one spot behind Fonty at the end of the season and two in front of Bob.

He finished fifth in the first race of the 1949 Strictly Stock series and ran in four other races of the fledgling eight-race series. He finished eighth in the series,

Tim Flock stands by his Hudson Hornet, 1953. (ISC Images & Archives via Getty Images)

with his best result being second on the beach at Daytona.

Two races into 1950, Tim joined his brother on NASCAR's winners' list, finishing just ahead of Bob and three laps clear of third on the track, Clyde Minter. He led for 153 of the 200 laps and stamped himself as a rising star, even though he did not win again that season.

In 1951, he won seven times in his 30 starts of the 41-race season and finished in third spot behind Herb Thomas (seven wins) and Fonty (eight wins), while Bob finished the season in the hospital with a broken neck from a crash that fortunately did not damage his spinal cord.

Then, in 1952, he started the season with a win in the opening race and went on to win another seven times, dominating the first 23 races of the 34-series. However, he had to hold off Herb Thomas, who won four of the final six races, to secure his first title. All Flock needed was to start the final race to have enough points, which was just as well since he ended the race on his lid after a crash on lap 164.

He later said he thinks he is the only driver to win a championship upside down.

While this story is not about a monkey, it is a story that must be told. It reveals more about Tim Flock, the man, rather than just Tim Flock the racer.

The season after his first title didn't start so well, so his car owner, Ted Chester, came up with the idea of running a rhesus monkey in the passenger seat while he was in a pet store buying a puppy for a family member's birthday present. He hoped it would have a twofold effect. The first was that other drivers might be distracted by a monkey looking at them as they diced with the champion, and the second was that it would likely give Flock a popularity boost while he recovered his mojo.

The monkey, known as Jocko Flocko, wasn't initially allowed into the track, so Flock had to smuggle him in for his debut race at Charlotte Speedway in April. The new pairing started on pole, and Jocko wasn't strapped into his seat until Flock was ready to race, cleverly sneaking him into the action, which surprised the rest of the field, who had no idea what was happening.

Tim Flock (#91) leads Curtis Turner (#41) during the NASCAR Cup race at Martinsville Speedway. (ISC Images & Archives via Getty Images)

The fans embraced Jocko, and NASCAR ultimately allowed him to race. "Jocko Flocko" was even written on the roof of the car like a driver's name.

In their sixth race the pair won at Hickory Speedway, NC, and that is the only time a driver and co-driver, let alone a monkey, has won a NASCAR race. It was also Flock's only win for the season.

Sadly, in Raleigh three races later, Jocko escaped from his harness and, while wandering around inside the car, found a trap door that drivers used to check tire wear and that didn't go well. That was Jocko's final race.

"We had this chain hooked onto the floorboard that we would pull up to check on the wear on the right front tire," Flock said in the book *Dirt Tracks To Glory: The Early Days of Stock Car Racing As Told By the Participants.* "Well, old Jocko had been watching me do that, and soon as he came unstrapped, he went right for the hole and stuck his head through. The tire zipped him on the head, and he liked to have went [sic]crazy."

Jocko was never the same, and he refused to eat and was eventually euthanized.

Despite the lack of success, the season was pretty full-on as he traveled the country with his "Fabulous Hudson Hornet" in tow. After a drive from Rochester, New York, to the

A worker posting Champion Sparkplug signs around the track, not seeing Flock, parked his truck on his head.

Piedmont International Fairgrounds in Spartanburg, South Carolina, a 12-hour drive today and probably close to 20 in 1953, he and Herb Thomas lay down for a sleep beside their cars in the infield.

A worker posting Champion Sparkplug signs around the track, not seeing Flock, parked his truck on his head. The driver panicked and six highway patrolmen lifted the truck off his head. He was taken to the hospital and missed six races.

If 1953 had been a season to forget, then 1954 somehow managed to sink even lower. He appeared to start strong, taking the win at Daytona in the second race of the season – only to be disqualified for using carburettor screws illegally. The victory was handed to Lee Petty, and Flock, furious at the ruling, walked away from NASCAR in protest. Ironically, his disqualified run still made history – it marked the first use of a two-way radio in a Grand National car.

Flock eventually returned to the series 30 races later, linking up with Buck Baker Racing. He made an immediate impact,

Tim Flock was the master of the Daytona Beach and Road Course, yet he only won the Grand National race there twice. In 1956, he won the race in the #300-A Chrysler. (Alamy)

finishing second in his comeback race, and subsequently competed in three of the final five events of the season.

Then came 1955 – and with it, redemption. Flock signed with Carl Kiekhaefer's newly formed team and took the wheel of the all-new Chrysler 300. What followed was one of the most dominant and controversial seasons the sport had seen. At Daytona, the fourth

round of the championship, Flock was again at the center of a headline-grabbing result – this time being declared the winner after Fireball Roberts was disqualified post-race. Whether poetic justice or pure irony, Flock was back on top.

Kiekhaefer's Chryslers raced with an automatic transmission, and while Strictly Stock, everything was optimized and replaced as often as needed. Some estimates had him spending 20 times as much as his rivals. The automatic initially lacked punch coming out of the

(L-R) Fonty Flock, Tim Flock, Bob Flock, and Herb Thomas pose for a publicity shot before a NASCAR Cup race at Raleigh Speedway. (ISC Images & Archives via Getty Images)

corners; however, as the team and driver began to understand it better, something special was unlocked.

Wins followed across the USA … New York, New Jersey, Pennsylvania, Michigan, California, Arizona, Alabama, and the Carolinas. Eighteen wins in all across 39 starts, a record only bettered by Richard Petty, who won 27 from 48 starts in 1967 and 21 from 46 races in 1971.

His series win was also by a considerable margin; 1508 points clear of Buck Baker.

While he was winning and making more money that he ever thought possible with both a significant wage, thanks to Chrysler, and the ability to keep all the prize money, he was struggling with Kiekhaefer's drill sergeant ways and after starting 1956 the way he finished 1955, with three wins from eight starts – including another Daytona – he abruptly quit the Kiekhaefer team after his victory in the Wilkes County 160 at North Wilkesboro Speedway.

Flock said he had ulcers from the stress of driving for Kiekhaefer, and that he needed to walk away from him while he still could. He cited rules from Kiekhaefer, such as the one that banned his drivers from sleeping in the same bed as their wives the night before a race, for which he hired extra motel rooms to accommodate.

"He would watch us all night to keep us apart, things like that got worse and worse," he said when talking about why he needed to leave a team that had brought him 21 wins in 46 starts.

Herb Thomas replaced him in the team, although he too quit before season's end, while Flock flicked through several teams for the rest of the season. He had one more win for his career on

Flock was a strong advocate for and a prime mover in attempting to establish a driver's union.

the road course at Road America (the first of three times the Cup Series raced on the iconic track, the others coming in 2021 and 2022), and then went into semi-retirement.

In his later years of racing, Flock was a strong advocate for and a prime mover in attempting to establish a drivers' union. Flock and Turner were the two leading players in what was known as the Federation of Professional Athletes, in association with the Teamsters Union. NASCAR didn't take kindly to this and threatened to ban any driver who joined.

When only Flock and Turner were left, they were "banned for life for conduct detrimental to auto racing." The bans were overturned in 1965, but Flock never raced again.

His career ended with an enviable record of a win in less than every five races, two championships, and a race win with a monkey as a co-driver. He was the *Speed Age* magazine Driver of the Year in 1952 and NASCAR's Most Popular Driver in the championship year of 1955.

Tim Flock with his trophy after winning the 1956 Daytona. (ISC Images & Archives via Getty Images)

He died in 1998 of throat and liver cancer before being posthumously inducted into the NASCAR Hall of Fame as one of its true characters.

Ned Jarrett was a two-time NASCAR Cup champion (1961 and 1965), scoring 50 Cup wins during a career which spanned the years 1952 through 1966. (ISC Images & Archives via Getty Images)

NED JARRETT

Birth date	October 12, 1932
Place of birth	Conover, North Carolina
Cup Series titles	2 (1961, 1965)
Competed between	1952–1966
Results	50 wins from 352 races

Ned Jarrett represented the next wave of NASCAR, the first great driver not to have started the first race at Charlotte in 1949. Making legend status was not as easy as with the first set of moonshine runners and mavericks, especially when you are calm and measured, unlikely to let fists fly, but more than willing to mix it up on the track. For a decade, "Gentleman Ned Jarrett" was a superstar of the growing sport.

Ned Jarrett's racing career started in 1952 under the pseudonym John Lence with a handful of stock car races. By the end of his career, his birth name was indelibly etched in NASCAR record books as a two-time champion and the winner of 50 races at the top level of NASCAR.

John Lence was Jarrett's brother-in-law's name, and with his father, Homer, forbidding him from racing he stumbled into it under the Lence name. Stock car drivers still carried a reputation tied to moonshining, and Homer had no interest in seeing his son follow that path. But racing was all Ned wanted. Working at the local sawmill with his father was just a job.

Though barred from driving, he was allowed to help work on the Ford Sportsman car he co-owned with Lence. One race day at nearby Hickory Motor Speedway, Lence fell ill and Jarrett seized the moment. He raced under Lence's name and finished second. He was 19, and the hook was set.

Ned Jarrett ran six of the eight NASCAR Convertible Series races he entered in his own 1957 Chevrolet during the 1959 season. (ISC Images & Archives via Getty Images)

For a while, he kept up the act, entering races under the assumed name. But when the wins started piling up, he couldn't hide the truth from his father any longer. Finally, Homer relented, and if his son was going to race, he might as well use his real name.

That decision began an extraordinary career – 50 Grand National Series wins, two Cup championships, and two more titles in NASCAR's second-tier division, now known as the NASCAR O'Reilly Auto Parts Series.

His first race in the Grand National Series was the following season, again at Hickory, with a follow-up race the next week at Darlington. He did two more races in 1954, three in 1955, two in 1956, and one in 1957.

He was second in the 1956 Sportsman Division Championship and then won the series in 1957 and '58. He wanted more, though; he wanted to race in the Grand National Series, and he believed he was good enough. It is reported that in that two-year period of the championship wins, he won 80 races, but he also had friendships tested.

Ralph Earnhardt – the father of Immortal Dale Earnhardt – and Jarrett were great friends and rivals in this era. The friendship was so strong that the Earnhardts even hosted a baby shower for Ned's wife, Martha – ironically, Earnhardt's wife was also Martha – the day after Earnhardt punted Jarrett into the fence to win a race at Gaffney Speedway. Jarrett drove his wife to the shower, but refused to go in. It took a good 12 months to mend the relationship.

What stung Jarrett that day wasn't the contact – it was the principle.

He knew rubbing was part of the trade. Expected it, even. But to Jarrett's mind, Earnhardt crossed the line. And what cut deeper was that Earnhardt wouldn't admit it.

Speaking at an evening meeting of the Eastern Lincoln Historical Society in 2018, Jarrett discussed the sport's tough early days and the tracks that challenged all drivers. Given that the tracks were mostly dirt ovals to start with, drivers had to battle dust and ruts, often making it tough not to hit others. But sometimes, he said, you wanted to hit them, given how narrow the tracks were.

"The only way you could pass another car was to knock it out of the way. That actually happened to me with Richard Petty. He was the one who knocked me out of the way."

Partway through 1959, the 1957 Ford in which Junior Johnson had won 11 Grand National races in a season and a half was put on the market by its owner, Paul Spaulding, who was making a switch to Dodge. Jarrett knew he could win in that car. He figured that, with no disrespect to Johnson, if Johnson could win with it, so could he.

He had guts, talent, and a plan – but nowhere near the $2,000 he needed to buy a race car. So, he did what any self-respecting racer would do: he backed himself.

With back-to-back races on deck – Saturday night at Rambi Raceway in Myrtle Beach and Sunday at the Southern States Fairgrounds in Charlotte – Jarrett wrote a check for the car. It was post-dated to Monday. If he didn't cover it, he was going to jail.

No pressure.

"I figured if I won both races, I'd be close enough to the money," Jarrett later recalled. "Then I'd hustle around and borrow the rest."

“The only way you could pass another car was to knock it out of the way.”
– *Ned Jarrett*

As reigning Sportsman champ, Jarrett was banking on a $100 appearance fee plus $800 per win. That meant $1,800 if it all went to plan – only $200 shy. Surely, he could scrounge the rest by Monday morning.

But there was a snag. He and crew chief Bud Allman picked up the car on Saturday morning and drove straight to Myrtle Beach. No time to prep. The foam-wrapped wheel was sealed with electrical tape wound in the wrong direction, creating tiny sharp edges that cut his hands to the bone.

Jarrett had raced at Rambi before. He knew the track, knew it would rut up under the weight of the cars. He and Allman devised a plan: run high, build a new groove, and wait.

For 100 laps, he played the long game, slowly carving out a line above the ruts. While others pounded the potholes, Jarrett sailed smoother. “It took 100 laps, but when it worked out,” he said later, “I set sail, unlapped myself, and lapped the field.”

He won. But he didn’t realize the steering wheel had sliced his hand open until after the race. It was bleeding so badly he needed a tourniquet to accept the trophy and the all-important check.

From there, it was straight to a hospital in Conway to get patched up, then back to Charlotte. No rest. The car had to be turned around overnight for Sunday’s fairground race. By the time the green flag dropped, Jarrett was running on pure fumes.

Halfway through, he couldn’t hang on any longer. He pitted and handed the car to Joe Weatherly. The problem was that Weatherly was too short to reach everything properly. So, when Junior Johnson blew his engine later in the race, Jarrett made a bold call – he called Junior over and put him back in his old car.

Three drivers. One car. One win.

It’s still the only time a top-tier NASCAR race has been won with a driver relay. But by the rules of the day, the driver who starts the race gets the credit. So, Jarrett, still bloodied and bandaged, was awarded the win.

Two races. Two victories. $1,800 in the bank. Jarrett tried to cut Weatherly and Johnson in on the winnings, but they waved him off. They knew the deal, and by Monday morning, with some borrowings, that post-dated check didn’t bounce and the stuttering career of Ned Jarrett was finally off and running.

However, those pair of wins were his only victories for the season, which ended with 17 Grand National races.

Still running the Ford, he won five times in 1960 from 40 starts. He was fifth in the series and won over $25,000.

Chevrolet decided to back Bee Gee Holloway's team in 1961 as a semi-factory outfit, and Holloway recruited Jarrett to lead the team. It took until the middle of the season for Jarrett to finally win in the Chev, taking out race 26 in the 52-race schedule at Birmingham International Raceway in Alabama.

In round 34 at Columbia Speedway, he finished third and took the points lead from 1960 champion Rex White, and 10 more finishes inside the top five without winning again gave him enough points to win his first title over White, who had won seven times.

At the end of the season, he sold his Chevrolet to Wendell Scott when he switched back to Fords for the next season. Scott was the third African American driver in NASCAR, but the first to be a regular driver in the Grand National Series, and the first to win a race, which he did in that car. There were still some pretty big racial divides in the early 1960s, so this was a significant decision by Jarrett, and is rated today as a measure of the man.

There were six wins in 1962, eight in 1963 and 15 in 1964 when he joined Bondy Long's team with direct support from Ford. It was also the first time he led the Grand National Series in wins, but Richard Petty was more consistent and won the first of his seven titles that year.

Ned Jarrett leads Fred Lorensen and Tiny Lund, who went on to win the 1963 Daytona 500. (Alamy)

At the Charlotte Speedway's famous World 600 that year, Jarrett had a coming together with Curtis Turner, and Fireball Roberts – so nicknamed because of his

After retiring, Jarrett turned his attention to racing promotion and broadcasting. (ISC Images & Archives via Getty Images)

fastball as a former pro-baseball pitcher – slammed into the spinning Ford of Jarrett. Roberts's car spun backward into the wall and flipped onto its lid and then exploded in flames.

Jarrett, whose car was also burning, was able to climb out of his stricken car and went straight over to Roberts, who was trapped in his Ford. It is reported from nearby fans that Roberts called out "My God, Ned, help me, I'm on fire." Roberts suffered second and third-degree burns, and the chemicals used to quash the fire affected his asthmatic respiratory system. Roberts survived for many weeks, and just when it looked like he was going to be OK, he contracted pneumonia and sepsis, slipped into a coma and died.

That made the season a tough one for Jarrett, but he was also dedicated to winning races and titles. Still with the Bondy Long team, and with the Hemi engines that powered Petty to the previous title now banned, the Ford Galaxy with a coil spring rear end and a 427 engine was the car to beat. And Jarrett's Galaxy, which he painted blue to match his wife Martha's eyes, was certainly among the best.

He started the 1965 season with three wins in the first eight races, including a win by 22 laps in the 200-lap race at Piedmont Interstate Fairgrounds in Spartanburg, South Carolina.

He also won the Southern 500 at Darlington by 14 laps, which is rated as one of the wildest races in NASCAR's history. Buren Skeen died during the race when he was driven into by two other cars after a spin. Cale Yarborough flew out of the track, rolled six times, and ended up in the car park while dicing for the lead. Then, others blew engines to try to keep up a winning pace. The eventual margin in the race was 19.15 miles, which is still the biggest win in NASCAR history.

A crash at Greenville-Pickens Speedway, North Carolina, in the middle of the season wrenched his back and bruised some vertebrae, leaving him to race the rest of the season with severe back pain.

He won 13 times, with six wins after the Greenville crash, and wrapped up his second title with a win in the final round at Dog Track Speedway in Moyock, North Carolina, which no longer exists. In reality though, he smashed the title in the middle of the season having traded the points lead with rookie Dick Hutcherson. He finished in the top five a staggering 42 times in 54 races.

Partway through 1966, Ford withdrew from NASCAR, and Jarrett only raced in 21 of the 49 races that season. At the age of 34, he decided that was enough for him, and he retired during the season, making him the only NASCAR champion to retire as a reigning champion. He finished third in his final race, which proved he still had it, too.

But that was it. He walked away and entered real estate before returning to NASCAR as part of the broadcast team after completing a course with Dale Carnegie. In 1991, that led to him calling his son, Dale's, first win in the Cup Series. Dale also became a NASCAR champion and was included in NASCAR's 50 Greatest Drivers in 1998, along with his father.

"Ned was as smooth and consistent as they came," Petty said. "They called him 'Gentleman Ned' for a reason. He didn't tear up equipment and he didn't push people around. He'd just outlast you. He won championships by being smart."

Petty related to Jarrett's strategy. "My dad used to say, 'Win the race as slow as you can.' Take care of the car. A lot of people thought Ned wasn't aggressive enough, but that was just smart racing."

Kyle Busch is perhaps the most divisive driver in this book; he's the one many love to hate . . . unless you love him, of course. (TaurusEmerald/Wikimedia Commons)

Kyle Busch

Birth date	May 2, 1985
Place of birth	Las Vegas, Nevada
Cup Series titles	2 (2015, 2019)
Competed between	2004–present
Results	63 wins from 678 races (as of end of 2024 season)

Kyle Busch didn't just enter NASCAR – he crash-tackled it like a punk rock act on a classical stage. From Vegas prodigy to double Cup champ, he's spent two decades proving that greatness doesn't always come with a polished smile but from grit and determination.

Kyle Busch is a heart-on-the-sleeve racer; fast, fiery, and never short on attitude he's been stirring the NASCAR pot since he first rolled onto pit road.

Love him or loathe him – and let's face it, if you're reading this book, you've probably done one or the other, or even both – Kyle Busch, also known as Rowdy, has built a career on speed, substance, and a stubborn refusal to care what anyone else thinks.

Ask Richard Childress, a man who famously tried to punch Kyle Busch after a 2011 Truck Series race at Kansas, furious over Busch's bump to RCR driver Joey Coulter. These days, Childress is the one paying him millions to drive. And now? He's a fan.

"Kyle Busch? He's not grumpy – he just wants to win. And I love that about him," Childress said. "After a tough qualifying night recently, he spent the next morning on the simulator, working, grinding – he wasn't giving up."

Busch joined RCR in 2023 after a long run at Joe Gibbs Racing. It was a seismic shift: the rowdiest man in the garage teaming up with the legacy Chevy squad once home to Dale Earnhardt. Eyebrows were raised.

But as ever, Rowdy let the results do the talking. A win at Auto Club Speedway in Fontana early in the season silenced the doubters and proved, once again, that Kyle Busch never lost his edge – he just changed his zip code.

"He's one of the best of all time," Childress adds. "And yeah, he's been a black hat, and the fans gave him hell for a while, but now that he's in a Chevrolet with RCR, I hear more cheers than boos."

And rightly so. With more than 230 wins across NASCAR's top three divisions, Busch has racked up stats that boggle the mind: 63 Cup Series wins, a record 102 in Xfinity, and 64 in Trucks. His dual championships in 2015 and 2019 tell only part of the story – he has won in every way, on every surface, in every car he's touched.

Kyle Busch's rocky relationship with fans is one of NASCAR's most fascinating long-running subplots, equal parts theater, ego, brilliance, and backlash. It's not that fans don't like Kyle Busch because he's not good. It's often because he's too good and refuses to apologize for it.

From the very start, Busch came in like a wrecking ball. He was brash, he was young, and he didn't care what people thought. He won early, he won a lot, and when he did, he celebrated like a villain straight out of central casting – burnouts, bows, and a smirk that said, "boo louder, I feed on it." That rubbed a lot of old-school fans the wrong way, especially in an era still mourning Dale Earnhardt and wary of NASCAR's youth movement.

Then there's the attitude. Busch never sugar-coated a bad day. He's flung microphones, stormed off from interviews, and made no secret of his frustration with rivals, officials, or even his own team. He is raw, which fans of more polished drivers see as arrogance. Fans of underdogs see him as the guy who stomped on Cinderella's slipper.

His signature bow after a race win isn't just a flourish – it's a Vegas-born spectacle with a smoky origin story. The tradition began early in his career during an Xfinity Series race at Charlotte. After executing a massive burnout that enveloped the track in smoke, Busch stepped out of his car to find the grandstands obscured. As the smoke cleared, he imagined himself as a magician emerging from a cloud, prompting him to take a theatrical bow to the crowd.

Kyle Busch leads the field en route to winning the NASCAR Sprint Cup Coke Zero 400 at Daytona International Speedway in 2008. (Alamy)

CAT
vertis
LOWE'S
ARMY
GUARD
JACK
ups

At age six, he got his first taste of racing – wheeling a homemade go-kart around the family's street while his father, Tom, managed the gas pedal. Kyle steered. Tom floored it. From that moment on, the fuse was lit.

Brother Kurt is seven years older and won a Cup Series crown in 2004. Both grew up spending more time in the family garage than at the dinner table. The pair learned the art of tuning cars, and Kyle became Kurt's dwarf car crew chief at just 10 years old. By 13, he was racing himself – and winning.

Between 1999 and 2001, Kyle Busch dominated the legends car scene at Las Vegas Motor Speedway – 65 wins, two track titles, and a growing reputation far beyond Nevada. In 2001, he jumped to late models and notched 10 wins in his rookie season.

Then came his NASCAR break. At just 16, Busch joined the Craftsman Truck Series, replacing Nathan Haseleu mid-

Kyle Busch during practice for the NASCAR Nextel Cup Pocono 500, 2005. (Nick Laham/Getty Images)

Kyle Busch celebrates a win at Texas Motor Speedway in 2020. (Alamy)

season in Roush Racing's #99 Ford. He finished ninth on debut at Indianapolis Raceway Park and nearly won his second start at Chicago, running out of fuel while leading.

He topped practice at Fontana but never raced – pulled due to a clash with a Marlboro-backed CART event. The 1998 Tobacco Master Settlement barred under-18s from tobacco-affiliated races, and NASCAR sidelined him. He ran six Truck races that year, with two ninth-place finishes, before NASCAR raised the minimum age to 18 because of its Winston backing.

With his NASCAR path temporarily blocked, Busch pivoted to the American Speed Association, finishing eighth in points. He also graduated early from Durango High and made his ARCA debut at Lowe's Motor Speedway, finishing 12th.

In 2003, he was withdrawn from his NASCAR debut even though he turned 18 during the season. NASCAR opted to withdraw him from the event out of caution, given the legal sensitivity around tobacco marketing and youth participation, even though he was now of legal age. He managed nine races in 2004 and then went full time in 2005.

Over 23 Cup seasons to date, Busch turned stats into sledgehammers: 63 wins, 252 top fives, 386 top 10s, 34 poles

Kyle Busch after winning the O'Reilly Auto Parts 500 at Texas Motor Speedway in 2018. (Bob Booth/Fort Worth Star-Telegram/Tribune News Service via Getty Images)

and a staggering 723 starts and nearly 20,000 laps led. He's completed just shy of 200,000 laps and banked more than $100 million in prize money.

He completed every race in a season 15 times and reeled off wins in 19 consecutive seasons before that bulletproof streak finally broke in 2024. He peaked statistically in 2008, winning eight races and frightening the field, but it was 2015 that delivered his championship dream, even after missing 11 rounds with a busted leg.

His 2015 season began with a broken leg and ended with a championship trophy. It all kicked off at the wrong place at the wrong time. On lap 112 of the Xfinity Series opener at Daytona, racing just outside the top 10, Busch got tangled in a wreck triggered when Erik

Jones and Kyle Larson touched coming off turn one.

Busch veered down the track, his #54 Toyota skidding across the apron. There were no SAFER barriers on the inside wall, just hard concrete. The impact was brutal – head-on at full noise, crushing the front end and breaking Busch's right leg and left foot in the blink of an eye. He climbed out himself, staggered, and collapsed.

It was the kind of crash that changes careers. Or ends them.

For weeks, it looked like Busch's 2015 was over before it began. He missed the Daytona 500. Missed the West Coast swing … 11 Cup races in total. While the Joe Gibbs Racing garage soldiered on without him, the paddock quietly wondered if Busch would ever come back.

But Busch didn't just recover – he reinvented his season.

In May, 11 weeks after the crash, he was back in the car at Charlotte Motor Speedway for the Coca-Cola 600. The return was emotional, but the results were slow to come – 19th at Charlotte, 36th at Dover. Then came Sonoma.

Busch rolled the dice on fuel strategy and won on a road course known for sorting the brave from the boys. It was his first victory since breaking his leg – and it wasn't a fluke. In the 10 races that followed, Busch won four more times, including back-to-back-to-back wins at Kentucky, New Hampshire, and Indianapolis.

It was the kind of crash that changes careers. Or ends them.

NASCAR tweaked its rules before the season, allowing drivers who missed time due to injury to remain playoff eligible if they won a race and finished in the top 30 in points. Busch ticked both boxes and roared into the Sprint Cup Chase.

And then, somehow, he did the unthinkable.

Busch put together a perfect race at Homestead-Miami Speedway, with the title on the line and Kevin Harvick breathing down his neck. He passed Brad Keselowski with 10 laps to go and never looked back. That night, just nine months after snapping bones at Daytona, Busch became a Cup Series champion and proved what he had always believed about himself – he wasn't just fast, he was also fearless.

His second Cup Series Championship in 2019 wasn't built on drama – it was built on dominance. After opening the season with four wins in the first 14 races, Busch went on a relentless run of 11 straight top 10 finishes, showing the consistency that breaks title rivals long before the finale.

Kyle Busch preparing for action in 2019. (Zach Catanzareti Photo, Wikimedia Commons)

While others had peaks and crashes, Busch quietly racked up points, leading the regular season and coasting through the playoffs without needing to win a race – until it mattered most. At Homestead, he was flawless on his way to victory lane and his second title.

In 2015, he won with heart. In 2019, he won with his head.

But Kyle Busch isn't just about numbers. He's about edge. Energy. Ego. All of it fused into one combustible, compelling package.

"I'm probably a sorer loser than he is," Childress admits. "But this sport needs that fire. You need a guy who doesn't give a damn what others think, who says, 'I'm here to win.' Kyle brings that. We've got too many vanilla drivers today – we need more like him."

He started early and made history early. At 19 years and 317 days, Busch became the youngest pole winner in Cup history (California, 2005). A year later, he was the youngest to make the Chase. By 2008, he gave Toyota its first Cup win. By 2015, he handed them their first Cup title.

The list of "firsts" is pure Busch: first to win two NASCAR national series races in the same day (Auto Club, 2009). First to sweep all three races (Truck, Xfinity, and Cup) in a single weekend (Bristol, 2010). Then he did it again. And in 2010, Kyle Busch Motorsports debuted in the Truck Series and won the owners' championship out of the gate. Eight wins. Job done.

But not all the numbers come with confetti. Busch has led the most laps in the Daytona 500 of any driver without a win in The Great American Race. It's a stat that screams both dominance and cruelty.

And then there was the end of an era. In 2021, M&M's and Mars walked away, closing the book on one of NASCAR's most iconic partnerships. Busch followed in 2022, announcing a blockbuster switch to Richard Childress Racing in 2023.

He's NASCAR's walking contradiction – the villain fans love to hate and the professional peers deeply respect. The Rowdy persona might be the headline, but behind the mask is one of the most detail-obsessed, technically sharp, and hard-working drivers in the garage.

As Drew Brown put it: "Kyle's our black hat, and he embraces it. But he's damn good. He's intense, driven, sometimes grumpy, but always entertaining. You don't need 43 Kyles – but you absolutely need one. The sport needs characters like him."

Kyle Busch launched the Kyle Busch Foundation in 2006 after visiting St. John's Home in Michigan, aiming to provide critical support for underprivileged children across the U.S. Two years later, he expanded his outreach with the "Kyle's Miles" program, partnering with Pedigree to aid shelter dogs and breed rescue groups.

He's about edge.
Energy. Ego.
All of it fused into one combustible, compelling package.

His charitable streak began even earlier – after his first Cup Series win at California in 2005, Busch and Rick Hendrick donated their winnings to Hurricane Katrina relief, a gesture he announced on *The Oprah Winfrey Show*, earning national praise.

Now 40, Busch is no longer the brash kid from Vegas. He's a father, a veteran, and still a fierce competitor. The wins keep coming. The fire still burns. And his story is far from over.

From teenage rebel to stat-sheet legend, Kyle Busch remains the lightning rod NASCAR didn't ask for – but absolutely needed.

In many ways, Red Byron is the first Immortal. He won the first NASCAR race and the first title, but that was it for the war hero. (ISC Archives/CQ-Roll Call Group via Getty Images)

Red Byron

Birth date	March 12, 1915; died November 11, 1960
Place of birth	Plasterco, Virginia
Cup Series titles	1 (1949)
Competed between	1949–1951
Results	2 wins from 15 races

Being the first is always a good way to etch your name in the annals of immortality, and such is the story of Red Byron. However, there is more to this World War II hero than just being the first champion of NASCAR; he was a great racer and innovator, as well as one of the sport's biggest personalities. He raced with an unlit cigar in his mouth and was a fierce competitor; he was one of the reasons people paid money to go to the races … one of the reasons NASCAR is what it is today.

Although born in Virginia, Robert Nold Byron – Bob to his family or Red to his mates thanks to that flock of Irish-Scottish red hair – turned into a bit of a nomad who eventually found himself in Alabama and Georgia as his career blossomed. He was mechanically inclined even at a young age. He spent much of his time at school devouring *Popular Mechanics* magazines and drawing racing cars and the like in the margins of his schoolwork.

He toyed with ways to build things that could go faster. A soapbox was not aerodynamic enough, so he engineered a smoother set of lines. However, this fascination brought him into conflict with his father, who wanted him to take his studies more seriously. Like many young racers of the day, he left the family home early to find his place in the world.

His family moved to Colorado, and his mother died when he was 10. His father, along with his father's new wife (his mother's sister), became even stricter with young Bob. He left home and worked as a coal miner south of Denver, living in the shadow of the famous Pikes Peak Hillclimb, which, while inspiring, was nothing on the stories he was hearing of the emerging stock car racing scene in the south.

He moved to Anniston, Alabama, just a stone's throw from a patch of land that was used for the Anniston Air Force Base in World War II and today houses the Talladega Superspeedway. He also started the Alabama Racing Association with a few other drivers. This was the beginning of a true grassroots motorsport community, where war veterans, bootleggers, and backyard mechanics all came together to test their skills and machines on hastily prepared dirt ovals. The camaraderie was raw and authentic – racing was a passion more than a profession, and everyone pitched in to keep the dream alive. It was here that Byron learned the unglamorous but vital arts of tuning engines under flickering shed lights and sleeping in truck beds between events.

He was 17 when he started racing and, a decade and a half later, won the first sanctioned NASCAR race in 1948 and then the first two titles handed out by the fledgling NASCAR organization, one of which is now known as the Cup Series. He, along with his team owner Raymond Parks, NASCAR's first team owner, played a significant role in the formation of the body that was eventually named NASCAR. Their success was no accident – it was built on mutual trust, mechanical genius, and Byron's dogged determination. Theirs was a partnership formed in the forge of struggle, ambition, and a shared belief in the future of stock car racing.

Pre-war, there were two distinct streams to stock car racing, one coming out of Georgia and the other out of Florida. The cars in Georgia were highly modified cars that were once used for moonshine running, and for much of the development of pre-war stock car racing, occasionally still used for that purpose. The Florida scene, centered around Daytona Beach, was more focused on land speed records and organized promotion. The convergence of these worlds created a crucible for what would soon become a national obsession, as blue-collar ingenuity met big-event spectacle.

After he moved to Atlanta, he became a member of what was known in racing circles as the Georgia Gang, despite not being a moonshine runner or criminal of any sort. He was a racer. But he raced among them, and against them, and was respected all the same.

Red Byron and a Raymond Parks-owned Ford V-8 was the winning recipe before the first Strictly Stock race in 1949. (ISC Images & Archives via Getty Images)

He was able to build cars he raced, and he understood racing and its strategy like few before or after him. He didn't care how many laps he led, so long as he led the last. He won his first significant race with a broken nose and a split lip that required 12 stitches after a crash earlier in the day. He cut his racing teeth on the red clay of the Piedmont, traveling from one race meeting to the next, cramming parts into the back of a pickup and sleeping in a makeshift tent when he couldn't afford a room. He lived lean and raced hard.

Racing the Flock family (fellow Immortal Tim, brothers Fonty and Bob,

and sister Ethel Mobley), Lloyd Seay, Roy Hall – all from the Georgia Gang – and Bill France from Florida, the sport started growing, and by 1939, it was the biggest sport in the South. Speedways were popping up throughout the region, struggling farmers built tracks, and fairgrounds became havens for speed, noise, and risk.

Racers like Byron became local celebrities, sought after by fans, car builders, and bootleggers who appreciated their driving prowess. He was never flashy off the track, preferring quiet evenings tinkering in the garage or poring over lap charts and gear ratios, but behind the wheel he was fearless. Courage wasn't just a byproduct of Byron's service – it was something baked into his DNA. His quiet discipline made him a different kind of hero – more engineer than entertainer, more tactician than daredevil.

Like the entire world, the U.S. was eventually dragged into World War II, and Byron enlisted early to try to become a pilot. However, the Air Force said his eyesight wasn't good enough and stuck him in the back of a plane to navigate and launch bombs.

Red Byron after another win in his Ford V-8. (Author's collection)

After each race, he was exhausted, but this was racing at the highest level.

On his 58th mission aboard a B-24 Liberator bomber over the Aleutian Islands in 1943, his plane was either shot down by a Japanese fighter plane or a bomb he was releasing went off early, and shards of metal ripped into his left leg and hip. The wounded plane limped its way back to safety, and Byron only just made it. He returned home with injuries that would end most careers before they started.

In a makeshift war hospital, doctors wanted to amputate the leg to improve his chances of survival, but he wouldn't let them since he knew that would end his racing career. Instead, he endured more than two years of torturous rehab, moving back to the new family home briefly before using some of his pension to buy an old Ford convertible and get mobile again.

He made it back to Atlanta and started to rebuild his racing career. Initially, he designed a hand clutch so he could change gears, and that worked well enough, and he started winning races. At the same time, he was also toying with open-wheelers and dreamed of winning the Indy 500, for which he tried but never qualified.

He had the race craft, but not the money to build a car fast enough to compete in that world.

Stock cars were a different story. Post-war, they were growing, and the money for winning races was on the rise. Byron also knew he needed more speed than he could build for himself, and for that he aligned with Louis Vogt – another "Red" – who built the fastest Ford V-8s in America for Raymond Parks.

Parks saw the emergence of stock car racing and put drivers in his cars and shared the purse with them. Parks first had to get his head around the crippled war veteran, but Vogt said Byron was the driver they needed to replace Seay, who had been murdered in 1941.

Red Byron, the "bespectacled, balding wounded war veteran," was one of its stars. With Vogt, they moved to a clutch pedal operation with "fatigue pins" to keep Byron's foot connected to the pedal and abandoned the hand clutch.

The device involved a stirrup arrangement. To change gear with his weakened leg, he needed to shift his body and use the leg brace to push the clutch. It was physical but effective. He never complained.

He was winning races in fast pre-war Ford V-8s. After each race, he was exhausted, but this was racing at the highest level. In 1946, he won

Shown in 1949, Red Vogt (left) wanted Red Byron (right) to drive the cars he was preparing for Raymond Parks. It was his genius that created the stirrup for the clutch, enabling Byron to race. (ISC Archives/CQ-Roll Call Group via Getty Images)

at Seminole Speedway and then on the beach at Daytona. Sitting in a bar after Daytona, he met Nell Davis, who became his wife.

In 1947, he raced 35 times and won 16 of the main races. That 46 percent winning rate has never been repeated or beaten. However, only 18 of those races were in France-sanctioned events, and he missed the title to Fonty Flock.

In December 1947, NASCAR was formed at Daytona Beach, and Byron was the drivers' representative. That made 1948 the first NASCAR season.

Byron was crowned NASCAR Modified Division Champion with 11 wins from 34 races, including the first NASCAR race at Daytona Beach.

On July 27, in Columbus, Georgia, Byron was dicing for the lead when he cut a tire and crashed into the crowd, injuring 17. Seven-year-old Roy Brannon died the next day.

This death left Byron hollow. But he kept racing, and kept winning, to claim the 1948 title. The final race of the season was in Columbus. Nell told her husband to "be careful, but to win."

Red Byron won the inaugural NASCAR Strictly Stock title in 1948 and then again in 1949. (ISC Archives/CQ-Roll Call Group via Getty Images)

He let Flock into the lead at halfway, but later pushed through the doubts and took back the lead and the title.

In 1949, Byron had a few wins before NASCAR launched the Strictly Stock class in the middle of the year. He cut ties with Parks, but later negotiated a better deal.

After a few experimental races, the first race of what became the Cup Series was held at Charlotte. Byron finished third in an Oldsmobile 88. He won the next race at Daytona.

The new series was proving popular. Byron won again at Martinsville and placed well at Langhorne, wrapping up the title.

He raced in six of eight races that year, winning two and finishing top five in two more. He earned 842½ points and went into the record books as the first NASCAR champion.

Injuries and the grind of longer seasons ended his career. He raced nine more times through 1950–51, finished in the top 10 five times, and then retired. He remained involved in racing and was working on an American car for Le Mans when he died in 1960 at age 44.

His impact on the sport, however, would long outlive him. Many of NASCAR's earliest stars would go on to become rich, famous, and celebrated, but Byron's influence was felt just as strongly through his quiet example of perseverance. He raced not to be a star, but because he loved it.

Red Byron was a pioneer not just for his success but for how he achieved it. His war injuries would have sidelined most people, but he adapted, innovated, and kept racing. He brought a level of mechanical understanding that influenced the way cars were tuned and prepared. His collaboration with Red Vogt set a template for driver–mechanic partnerships that carried on into future generations of the sport.

He also set a cultural tone within the paddock. Byron was respected not only because he was fast but because he was thoughtful. Other drivers listened when he spoke, knowing his insights were built on experience and hardship. He was one of the early voices pushing for better treatment of drivers, including fairer purses and safety considerations.

NASCAR itself owes much of its early legitimacy to Red Byron. Winning the first ever NASCAR-sanctioned race, then becoming the first Modified Champion and first Strictly Stock (Cup Series) Champion gave the fledgling organization the credibility it needed to grow. Byron's name lent weight to what could have remained a regional curiosity but instead became a national institution.

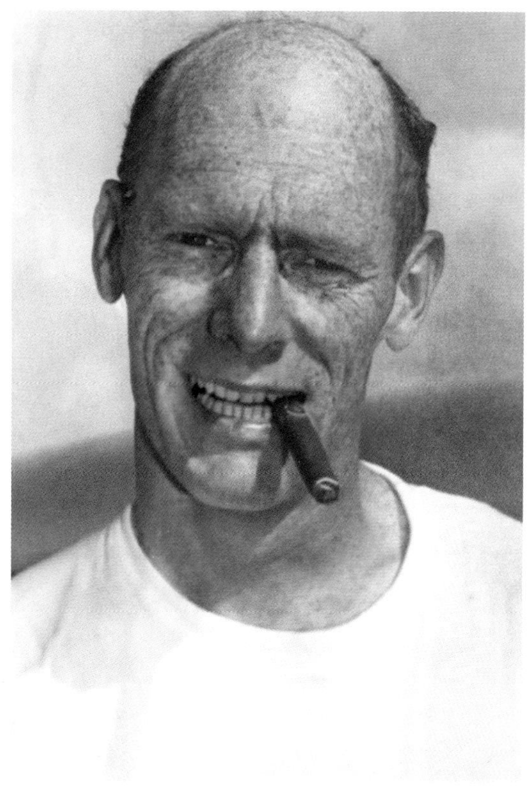

Despite his war injuries, Byron went on to fame in NASCAR. (ISC Images & Archives via Getty Images)

His post-racing ambitions spoke to his endless curiosity and drive. Designing an American car to win at Le Mans was no small dream – it showed that Byron was thinking globally before it was fashionable. He saw no reason that American engineering and driving couldn't succeed on the world stage. One wonders what he might have achieved had he lived longer.

Today, his legacy lives on in museums, in Hall of Fame plaques, and in the stories passed down by those who knew him. But perhaps his greatest legacy is spiritual: the reminder that no obstacle is insurmountable when paired with determination, ingenuity, and heart. Red Byron didn't just make NASCAR history – he made NASCAR possible.

"He lived for it. He loved his racing," his daughter Bette Byron said. "It wasn't just a job to him. It was his life. I think he was very proud of that. I wish like heck he had lived long enough to see how much it has grown."

One title doesn't fully capture Bobby Allison's impact on NASCAR . . . 85 wins make a bigger statement. (Robert Alexander/Getty Images)

Bobby Allison

Birth date	December 3, 1937; died November 9, 2024
Place of birth	Miami, Florida
Cup Series titles	1 (1983)
Competed between	1961–1988
Results	85 wins from 718 races

Bobby Allison, like so many of the Immortals, lived life on the edge. A tough and uncompromising racer who didn't take a backward step on or off the track. His fight with Cale Yarborough brought national attention and fame, but it was on the track where his legend was forged as the leader of the "Alabama Gang."

When Bobby Allison stopped to check on his brother, Donnie, who had wrecked on the final lap of the 1979 Daytona 500, he shot to national fame. Donnie had crashed with Cale Yarborough, and when Bobby stopped to check his brother was OK and offer him a lift back to the pits, Yarborough rushed up to the #15 car and blamed his championship rival for the crash and then swung his helmet at Bobby.

With a cut nose and split lip, Bobby fired back and soon fists, feet, and helmets were flying. To be fair, this sort of skirmish was not uncommon in most levels of NASCAR, but this was the first time the race was broadcast live on national TV, and the footage of the fight dragged NASCAR onto the front page and into the minds of sports fans.

Reflecting on the chaos years later, Bobby Allison told *Secret Base* in 2010, "The thing was really unusual." Though Donnie had been wrecked out of a possible win, Bobby had stayed focused on finishing the race, but once he saw the confrontation unfold, he knew he had to "address the situation."

He was known for being fiercely independent. He wasn't afraid to speak his mind, take on bigger teams, or call out inequities in the sport.

As he put it with a grin, "He hit me in the face with his helmet ... then he went to beating on my fists with his nose."

In the aftermath, NASCAR fined all three men involved, Bobby, Yarborough, and Donnie, with Bobby's fine alone outweighing his race earnings. His wife, Judy, had to write a check from home just to get them to the next event. But in the grander scheme, the whole mess helped make NASCAR a household name.

Allison, already with 57 wins at that time, was now a well-known name who would win the Cup Series for the first and only time four years later. Winning only one felt a little slender as a return for this larger-than-life racer, but he was runner-up another five times.

He was 17 when he ran his first race, which required parental permission, which was given by his mother, who hoped one race would be enough. After finishing school, he moved to Wisconsin to work with his mother's brother-in-law, Jimmy Hallet, at Mercury Outboard Motors. His mother thought this would take him away from motor racing, but Carl Kiekhaefer owned Mercury, and he also owned a NASCAR team.

Her attempt to sidetrack his racing desire had the opposite effect. Kiekhaefer was notoriously hard to work with, and he returned to Miami after a couple of months, having attended 19 races, all of which were won by Kiekhaefer cars.

Back in Miami, and with his parents forbidding him from racing, he did what many others did at the time: he raced under a fake name, in his case, Bob Sunderman. After winning a race, his face appeared in a local newspaper, and the charade was done; his parents reluctantly accepted his choice.

That choice took him to Alabama with brothers Donnie (a racer) and Eddie (who turned spanners on race cars) to chase more lucrative short tracks. Here, in Hueytown, he became a key member of the legendary "Alabama Gang," which formed around the brothers, Neil Bonnett, and Charles "Red" Farmer.

With numerous speedways paying good money, he started to build a career.

His NASCAR debut was in 1961 at the wheel of a Ralph Stark Chevy, and he finished 20th in his qualifying race at Daytona and 31st in the main event, which was won by Marvin Panch and had 58 starters. There were only two more

Bobby Allison was leading the 1969 Daytona 500 when the engine blew in his Mario Rossi-owned Dodge Charger and he spun in the oil on lap 45. (ISC Images & Archives via Getty Images)

races that season, and he showed nothing spectacular in speed or form.

It took until 1965 to get another run at the top level, and while running his own car for the first half of the 1965 season, he achieved a pair of top 10 finishes and placed 11th in the Daytona 500. He also finished seventh while driving for Ed Grady. Swapping teams was quite regular and easy back then, and each season up until 1972, he drove for multiple team owners, including some legendary figures like Smokey Yunick, Bob Moore, and John Moore/Ralph Moody.

It was driving for the more obscure JD Bracken team that he scored his first win at Oxford Plains Speedway, a feisty 0.375-mile speedway in Maine. He backed up four days later on another short track (Islip Speedway, the shortest track in the history of the Grand National/ Cup Series) and then a little more than a month later, a third win (another short track, this time the half-mile Beltville Speedway).

In six weeks of racing above and below the Mason-Dixon line, Allison had stamped himself as a legitimate contender and he finished 10th in the series from 33 starts of a possible 49. He then won thrice for Bracken in 1967 and once for "Cotton" Owens. He drove for five teams in 1967, four in 1968 and three in 1969, adding to his win tally each season.

It wasn't until 1970 that he ran a full campaign with 46 of 48 races, again across four different teams. He won three

Car owner Bill Ellis (left) talks with driver Bobby Allison (right) at a Cup race in the late 1960s. (ISC Images & Archives via Getty Images)

times and was runner-up in the series. In 1971, he won 11 times, including five in a row and his first of three World 600 wins at Charlotte, across two teams (his own and Holman-Moody) and driving Mercurys and Dodges.

This constant swapping of teams and cars kept him from winning more titles, according to Richard Petty, who admired Allison: "There was no more determined person than Bobby. But Bobby was his own worst enemy. He'd get to running good and then he'd decide he didn't like to work with these people, and he'd go out on his own, go broke again, and have to go back.

"He'd have won a lot more races and titles if he just stayed with a couple of good owners. But he always portrayed himself as the underdog. I wouldn't say he had an inferiority complex, but he just felt like everybody was against him or he was against everybody."

For Allison, it was a decade marked by consistency and grit, as he drove for numerous teams and often built or helped set up his own cars – a testament to his mechanical know-how and work ethic.

He was known for being fiercely independent. He wasn't afraid to speak his mind, take on bigger teams, or call out inequities in the sport. While this sometimes put him at odds with NASCAR's leadership, it earned him deep respect from fellow drivers and fans. He was the "blue-collar" driver, and when he started winning lots of races, he became the most popular driver in the series, winning the official popularity award from 1971–73 and then again from 1980–84.

Although Allison had been a title contender throughout the 1970s, the elusive championship finally came in 1983, when he won the NASCAR Winston Cup Series title at age 45. Driving for DiGard Racing, Allison combined veteran savvy with race-winning speed, outlasting a strong field to claim his first and only championship.

With 85 wins leading to only one title, there were plenty of other reasons to celebrate, like the three Daytona 500 victories: in 1978, 1982, and 1988. The 1988 win was especially emotional, as he beat his son, Davey Allison, to the finish line in a 1–2 family finish. That moment, captured in front of a roaring crowd, remains one of the most heartwarming scenes in NASCAR history.

Bobby Allison celebrates in the winner's circle after winning the Daytona 500 in 1988. (Alabama Digital Archives)

His other major wins include the other two big-ticket items, the Southern 500 at Darlington and the World 600 at Charlotte. He even won the first NASCAR race outside of North America at the Calder Park Thunderdome in Melbourne, Australia, which is where I first met him.

Through the glory came some disappointments and big crashes. Two big ones near the end of his career shook both Allison and the sport.

In 1987, he was driving a Buick LeSabre for DiGard Motorsports at

Bobby Allison topped his son, Davey, by two car lengths in the 1988 Daytona 500. It was only the second time in NASCAR Cup Series history that a father–son finished one–two. Lee and Richard Petty did it in 1960. The win was Allison's last in the Cup series. (ISC Archives/CQ-Roll Call Group via Getty Images)

Talladega. During the race, a tire failure caused his car to spin and become airborne at more than 200 mph. The car flew into the catch fencing near the start-finish line, tearing down a significant section and nearly entering the spectator area.

The crash didn't seriously injure spectators, but it sent shockwaves through the sport. With Allison's significant push, the crash led NASCAR to implement the restrictor plate rule the following year to limit speeds at superspeedways like Talladega and Daytona.

A little over a year later, one of the most decorated careers in NASCAR ended abruptly in June 1988, just months after his final Daytona 500 win and Calder Park trip.

Just after the start of the Miller High Life 500 at Pocono Raceway, Allison's

Bobby Allison did it all with heart. He wasn't just a great driver – he was a working-class hero in a fire suit. The last of the blue-collar racers.

car suffered a mechanical failure – believed to be a blown tire – causing it to spin and get struck at high speed by Jocko Maggiacomo. The impact was so severe that Allison's car was nearly torn in half. He suffered serious head injuries, including brain trauma, and was airlifted to the hospital. Although he recovered, the crash effectively ended his driving career.

He finished his career with 84 wins, but now has 85 in a curious twist of delayed justice. Among the many highlights of his Hall of Fame career, this belated 1971 victory at Bowman Gray Stadium – AKA The Madhouse – remains a gritty little gem.

Originally, Allison had crossed the finish line first in the 250-lap race but was disqualified in post-race inspection after officials ruled that his car had an illegal intake manifold. However, Allison and his team maintained that the part was within the rules, and the penalty remained a source of controversy for decades. In 2015 – 44 years later – NASCAR finally revisited the decision and reversed the disqualification, officially crediting Allison with the win.

Post career, tragedy struck again when his sons Clifford (practice crash) and Davey (helicopter crash) – both promising racers – were killed in separate incidents in the early 1990s. Despite his personal losses, Bobby Allison remained an enduring ambassador for the sport, always gracious with fans and deeply admired in the NASCAR community.

"Bobby was determined, no doubt," said Petty. "But he could be his own worst enemy."

Petty respected Allison's grit but noted, "He always saw himself as the underdog, even when he wasn't. That chip on his shoulder sometimes worked for him – but sometimes didn't."

Whether he was building engines in his garage, trading paint at Talladega, or celebrating in victory lane with his son, Bobby Allison did it all with heart. He wasn't just a great driver – he was a working-class hero in a fire suit. The last of the blue-collar racers.

Driver Bill Elliott holds the winning trophy after the Pennzoil Freedom 400, part of the NASCAR Winston Cup Championship Series at Homestead-Miami Speedway, Florida, in 2001. (Jon Ferrey/Allsport via Getty Images)

Bill Elliott

Birth date	October 8, 1955
Place of birth	Dawsonville, Georgia
Cup Series titles	1 (1988)
Competed between	1976–2012
Results	44 wins from 828 races

Bill Elliott's rise to superstardom wasn't just about speed – it was about connection. He didn't need to be loud or brash to earn the love of millions; he simply had to be himself. "Awesome Bill from Dawsonville" was NASCAR's Most Popular Driver for a record 16 seasons and that is what makes him an Immortal of NASCAR.

Dawsonville, Georgia. A small and quiet town nestled 90 minutes north of Atlanta with a population of less than 5,000. Blink, and you might miss it – unless, of course, you happen to be a NASCAR fan. Then Dawsonville takes on a mythical quality, a place where legends are born and sirens sang whenever victory was in the air.

At the heart of that legend is William Clyde Elliott – better known to the world as "Awesome Bill from Dawsonville." For nearly four decades, Bill Elliott was not only one of the fastest drivers in NASCAR but also one of its most beloved. His career wasn't forged in the boardrooms of big sponsors or the sprawling workshops of powerhouse teams. It was built in a speed shop turned Ford dealership, on red clay backroads and short ovals, and in the hearts of fans who saw something of themselves in a soft-spoken Georgian with a need for speed.

The Elliott family's rise was a distinctly American motorsport story. In the late 1960s, George Elliott – a passionate local racer and diehard

Ford man – began building and fielding cars in Georgia's Sportsman series. As time went on, his humble Dawsonville speed shop grew into a Ford dealership, and he redirected his attention toward supporting the racing dreams of his three sons: Ernie, Dan, and Bill.

Ernie became the mechanical mastermind, crafting potent engines that would soon terrorize superspeedways. Dan took the reins of the business side. Bill, the youngest, quietly honed his craft behind the wheel – gaining experience, if not results, through the late 1970s. The trio worked for Elliott Racing, a family-run effort that debuted on the Cup Series stage in 1976 with Bill behind the wheel.

In those early days, their Ford Torino was underpowered and outdated. They were short on budget, long on effort. But their fortunes began to turn when they acquired a used Mercury Montego that had once belonged to NASCAR star Bobby Allison. Suddenly, the underdogs had teeth. Bill started posting top 10 finishes, culminating in a runner-up spot to David Pearson in the 1979 Southern 500 at Darlington – one of NASCAR's toughest tests.

That race marked a turning point. Elliott's raw speed and fluid style on high-speed ovals drew attention. And just as importantly, so did his character: calm, polite, and focused. In an era where personalities like Darrell Waltrip and Dale Earnhardt dominated headlines with bravado and brawn, Elliott was the stoic contrast – a racer who let his driving do the talking.

Enter Harry Melling, a wealthy businessman from Michigan and sponsor who saw potential in the Dawsonville outfit. What began as a $500 deal blossomed into full-season support. In 1982, Melling bought the team from George Elliott and formally rebranded it as Melling Racing. It gave Bill the backing he needed to chase NASCAR glory full time.

Elliott's breakout came at the final race of the 1983 season at Riverside Raceway, where he scored his first Cup Series win. That same year, he finished third in the points standings, validating the potential many had seen in him.

The following year, Elliott claimed three victories and won NASCAR's Most Popular Driver award for the first of 16 times. He was beginning to connect with fans on a deeper level. Unlike the sport's more flamboyant stars, Elliott was a quiet, respectful Southern racer who hadn't changed a bit despite the rising fame.

1985 was the year that turned Elliott into a national sensation. NASCAR introduced the "Winston Million" bonus, offering a staggering $1 million prize to any driver who could win three

Bill Elliott's McDonald's Ford Thunderbird (#94) leads Dale Jarrett (#88) at Daytona International Speedway in the late 1990s. (ISC Images & Archives via Getty Images)

of the sport's four crown jewels: the Daytona 500, Winston 500 (Talladega), World 600 (Charlotte), and Southern 500 (Darlington).

Elliott wasted no time. He won the Daytona 500 in dominant fashion, then triumphed at Talladega with a remarkable comeback after starting from pole. After an early pit stop to repair a broken oil fitting left him nearly two laps behind, Elliott returned to the track and began an extraordinary charge. Without the aid of caution flags or drafting partners, he consistently ran laps near 205 mph, making up the lost distance under green flag conditions – a feat nearly unimaginable today with restrictor plates limiting top speed.

He said after the race all he could do "was go as fast as possible and hope it held together," which it did.

His speed on superspeedways was almost otherworldly, and he said in those days before restrictor plates, when you went out for qualifying, you weren't sure if you were returning. Ernie was

Bill Elliott prior to the start of the 1984 Daytona 500 stock car race. (Robert Alexander/Getty Images)

building the best engines in the field for superspeedways like Talladega, and Bill was making the most of it, turning lap after lap on the edge.

In 100 laps he had pegged back the two-lap deficit and then 23 laps later he reclaimed the lead on lap 145, briefly ceded it to Cale Yarborough, and then surged ahead for good on lap 169, ultimately winning by 1.72 seconds over Kyle Petty. Only three drivers finished on the lead lap. To this day, it is still rated by many as the greatest individual drive in NASCAR history.

A mechanical failure in the World 600 threatened his shot at the million, but he returned with a vengeance at Darlington, where he held off the field to capture the Southern 500 and the $1 million check. Only Jeff Gordon would match that feat before the program was retired in 1997.

From then on, "Million Dollar Bill" was etched into NASCAR lore.

The 1980s were a golden era for Elliott. His Ford Thunderbirds were aerodynamic rockets while drivers in other cars complained about how hard his car was to follow. He won races on superspeedways, short tracks, and road courses. He finished third in the championship in 1983 and '84 and was runner-up in 1985 – when he won 11 races all on superspeedways, had 11 pole positions and led more than 1000 laps more than Darrell Waltrip who won the title – and '87 before finally capturing the elusive NASCAR Cup Series Championship in 1988, although that nearly didn't happen.

In November 1987, just days after winning the final NASCAR race of the season in Atlanta, Elliott narrowly avoided tragedy during a promotional flight with the U.S. Air Force Reserve. While flying as a passenger in an F-16 fighter jet, Elliott's aircraft collided mid-air with an F-15 during a simulated combat maneuver.

The collision severely damaged the F-15, forcing its pilot to eject, while the F-16 with Elliott sustained significant damage to its right wing and fuel tank. Despite the damage and loss of communication, the F-16's pilot managed to land the aircraft safely. Unbeknownst to Elliott at the time, his ejector seat was not properly charged; had an ejection been necessary, it would have failed.

But he survived and in the 1988 season Elliott outlasted fierce rivals like Rusty Wallace and Dale Earnhardt to clinch the title by 24 points. It was the culmination of years of hard work – and a moment of validation for the small-town family that had dared to dream big.

> He was beginning to connect with fans on a deeper level. Unlike the sport's more flamboyant stars, Elliott was one of them – a quiet, respectful Southern racer who hadn't changed a bit despite the rising fame.

He won six races that season and had the same number of poles. He had more fruitful seasons than this one, but with a second place at Bristol in the 20th race of the season, he wrestled the lead in the series from Waltrip and wasn't headed from there.

His performance wasn't just about victories. It was about consistency, poise under pressure, and grace in the spotlight. Elliott proved that success didn't require theatrics; it required heart.

Bill Elliott's career was intertwined with some of NASCAR's most legendary rivalries.

With Dale Earnhardt, the contrast couldn't have been starker. Earnhardt – the gruff, aggressive "Intimidator" – was everything Elliott wasn't. Their clashes

Bill Elliott (#9) and Bobby Allison (#22) make up the front row as the field gets set for the start of the Winston 500 NASCAR Cup race at Alabama International Motor Speedway in 1987. (ISC Images & Archives via Getty Images)

defined the 1980s, none more so than the infamous 1987 All-Star Race, where Earnhardt's "Pass in the Grass" and subsequent victory left Elliott fuming.

On the surface, it was vintage Dale Earnhardt: bold, fearless, and untouchable. But for Bill Elliott, the other half of that infamous incident, the moment was less folklore and more farce.

The flashpoint came on the frontstretch at Charlotte Motor Speedway. Elliott, fast and hunting for the lead, pulled alongside Earnhardt, and the two made contact. Earnhardt veered into the grass, somehow held on, and rocketed back onto the track without losing position. The crowd erupted. The legend was born. But Elliott wasn't celebrating.

To him, it wasn't a pass – it was a byproduct of dirty driving. Elliott, running second, nudged Earnhardt after a hard block, but instead of Earnhardt being penalized or seen as vulnerable, the media flipped the script. The phrase "Pass in the Grass" entered NASCAR lore, despite there being no actual pass, and the narrative crowned Earnhardt the master of chaos. Elliott, meanwhile, was left stewing – not only about the lost race but about how the entire exchange had been romanticized.

Elliott would later say, "He didn't pass anybody in the grass. He was getting pushed there. That's not

"The King" Richard Petty with NASCAR's most popular driver, Bill Elliott, in 2009. (Alamy)

a pass – it's just Dale being Dale." What frustrated Elliott most wasn't the contact itself – it was that reckless defense was being repackaged as brilliance. To him, it represented a broader tolerance within NASCAR for Earnhardt's aggressive style, a style that clashed with Elliott's more methodical, rule-respecting approach.

The bitterness lingered. After the race, Elliott didn't hide his anger. He gave Earnhardt's car a retaliatory shot on the cool-down lap, a rare glimpse of fire from a driver known more for quiet focus than confrontation. In that moment, Elliott's frustration wasn't just about a race – it was about a sport seemingly celebrating spectacle over standards.

The tension was real, but so was the mutual respect that grew in later years.

With Rusty Wallace, the 1988 title duel was a battle of endurance. Wallace pushed hard in the closing rounds, but

Elliott's steady hand won out. Theirs was a rivalry built more on racing skill than fiery emotions.

And then there was Darrell Waltrip – media-savvy, polished, and frustrated by Elliott's surge in fan popularity. Waltrip won more races, but Elliott consistently beat him in the Most Popular Driver polls.

But perhaps Elliott's most consistent rival wasn't a person at all – it was the clock. His qualifying laps at Daytona and Talladega in 1987 were so fast (including a record 212.809 mph at Talladega) that NASCAR had no choice but to introduce restrictor plates to slow cars down. Elliott was often untouchable in a sport measured in seconds, on superspeedways.

Elliott's dominance faded as the 1990s wore on, though his popularity remained unwavering. He formed his own team in 1995 and later joined Evernham Motorsports in the early 2000s, where he found a second wind. His 2001 victory at Homestead – his first in seven years – was a fairytale comeback that fans celebrated nationwide.

Elliott stepped away from full-time racing in 2003 but made occasional starts into the next decade. In time, the

Bill Elliott (#9) challenges Jimmy Spencer (#26) at the start of the Brickyard 400 at the Indianapolis Motor Speedway. (Jonathan Ferrey/Allsport via Getty Images)

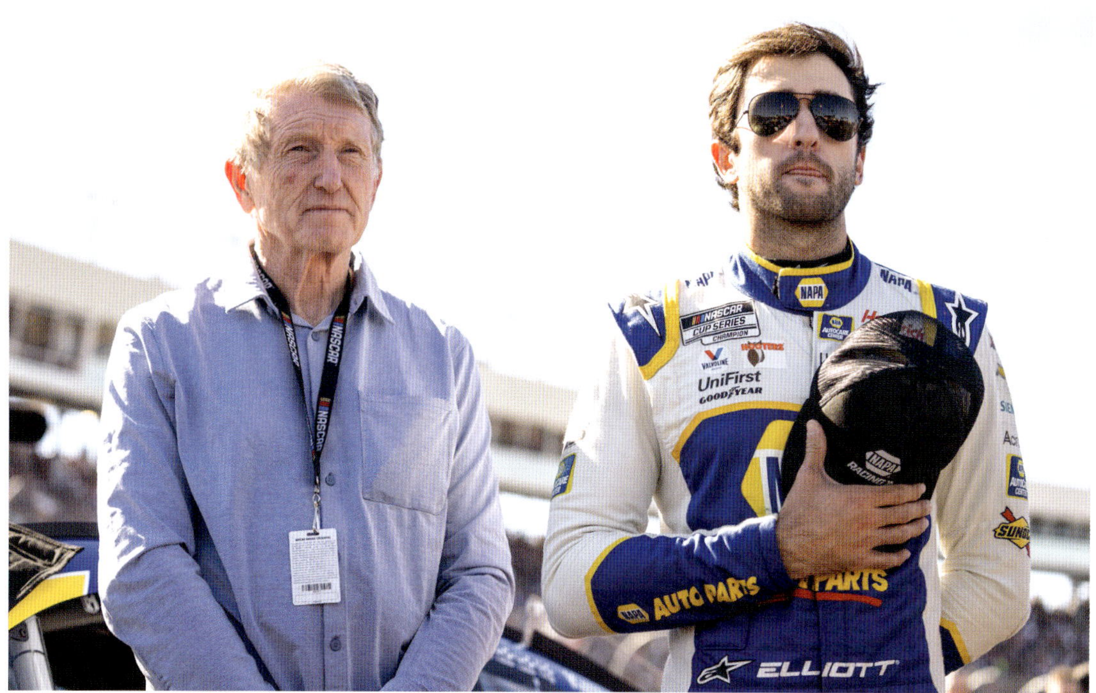

Bill Elliott (left) with son Chase Elliott in 2022, who is taking on the family tradition as a seven-time winner of the Cup Series' Most Popular Driver award. (Alamy)

torch passed to his son, Chase Elliott. Bill's influence was unmistakable – Chase carried himself with the same humility and determination that defined his father's career.

When Chase won the NASCAR Cup Series Championship in 2020, it was a proud moment for the Elliotts, who joined the Pettys and Jarretts as one of only three father-son duos to win NASCAR titles.

More than anything, Bill Elliott's legacy is defined by his connection to the fans.

He never chased fame or played the part of a showman. He simply showed up, raced hard, and signed every autograph in the line. He sounded like the fans. He lived like the fans. And when he won, the siren at the Dawsonville pool room blared in celebration, turning a small-town tradition into a national symbol.

Elliott stood out in an age of polished media images and corporate personas by not standing out. He was, and remains, authentic.

Kyle Larson is one of the most versatile racers in the world, and NASCAR is his prime playground. (Zach Catanzareti Photo/Wikimedia Commons)

Kyle Larson

Birth date	July 31, 1992
Place of birth	Elk Grove, California
Cup Series titles	2 (2021, 2025)
Competed between	2013–present
Results	24 wins from 348 races (as of end of 2024 season)

Kyle Larson is the most complete driver of his generation – a dirt-track natural turned NASCAR champion who can win in anything with wheels. From redemption to domination, his story isn't just about speed – it's about rewriting the rulebook on what a modern racer can be.

Few drivers on the planet match Kyle Larson for sheer range. Sprint cars, stock cars, sportscars – dirt, pavement, road courses, ovals, you name it. If it's got four wheels and a motor, Larson will find the edge and flirt with the limit. He's the guy other drivers call "a natural," even when he's lapping them.

I have to admit from the start of this chapter, I am a huge fan. I believe he is perhaps the best racer on the planet. He'd win if you stuck him in Formula 1 with the right car.

And unlike the other two modern-day giants in this book, Larson doesn't divide opinion. He's universally respected. Hell, even NASCAR bent the rules for him, tweaking the playoff system in 2024 so he could still qualify despite missing the World 600. Why? Because he was too busy racing the Indy 500. That's peak Larson: chasing greatness everywhere, all at once.

In 2025 alone, on his way to a second Cup Series title, he came agonisingly close – twice – to pulling off a weekend sweep, winning two out of three in Cup, Xfinity, and Truck across the same meet … finishing second in the other races.

Of course, his legend didn't start in NASCAR. Larson has dominated dirt racing since day one, racking up wins in all the heavy hitters. And when he turned his eye to endurance, he bagged a win at the 24 Hours of Daytona in 2015 with Chip Ganassi Racing. Different car, different surface, same result: Larson wins.

I caught up with him last year at the World of Outlaws opener at Volusia Speedway, just a week out from the Daytona 500, and a winning weekend. No fuss, no entourage, just a bloke who loves racing in 80-plus events a year. Sometimes two or three a week. NASCAR might be his main gig, but calling it his only job is like calling Bruce Springsteen a karaoke act.

Born on July 31, 1992, in Elk Grove, California, Kyle Larson's racing journey began almost immediately, attending his first race just a week after birth. By age seven, he was already competing in outlaw karts, quickly ascending through the ranks of open-wheel dirt racing. His early career was marked by significant achievements, including victories in prestigious events like the Kings Royal, Knoxville Nationals, and the Chili Bowl Nationals. In 2011, Larson made history by sweeping all three USAC divisions – midget, sprint, and silver crown – at the 4-Crown Nationals at Eldora Speedway, a feat that underscored his exceptional versatility and skill.

Chip Ganassi Racing recognized his prodigious talent and signed Larson to a developmental deal in 2012. That same year, he competed in the NASCAR K&N Pro Series East, securing two wins and the series championship, along with Rookie of the Year honors. In 2013, Larson transitioned to the NASCAR Nationwide Series (now NASCAR O'Reilly Auto Parts Series) with Turner Scott Motorsports, earning nine top five and 17 top 10 finishes, which led to him being named the series' Rookie of the Year.

In 2013, he dipped his toes into the Cup Series with Phoenix Racing, making his debut at Charlotte Motor Speedway in the #51 car. Starting 21st, his race was cut short by an engine failure, resulting in a 37th-place finish. A subsequent outing at Martinsville ended similarly, with another engine issue relegating him to 42nd.

The following year, Larson took the wheel of the #42 Chevrolet for Chip Ganassi Racing as a full-time Cup Series driver. His rookie season showcased raw talent and potential, highlighted by 17 top 10 finishes and a second-place run at Auto Club Speedway. Despite a few rookie missteps, including a notable incident at Michigan where a block on

Tony Stewart led to on-track tensions, Larson's performance earned him the 2014 NASCAR Sprint Cup Series Rookie of the Year award, boasting a higher top 10 finish rate than legends like Richard Petty and Jeff Gordon during their debut seasons.

In 2015, Larson's momentum faced challenges. A fainting episode at Martinsville led to a missed race, and while he secured a few top 10 finishes, he ended the season 19th in points, still seeking his first Cup win.

That elusive victory came in 2016 at Michigan International Speedway, where Larson broke through after 99 starts, an emotional and career-defining moment. This win secured him a spot in the Chase, though he was eliminated in the Round of 16.

The 2017 season marked Larson's breakout. He won four races, including a dramatic victory at Michigan, where he executed a four-wide pass on the final restart. He led 1,352 laps that year and finished eighth in the standings.

Kyle Larson in August 2021. (Zach Catanzareti Photo, Wikimedia Commons)

Driving the #42 Chip Ganassi Racing Chevy at Fontana Speedway in 2020. (Alamy)

In 2018, consistency kept him in playoff contention, but victory lane remained out of reach. Despite leading 284 laps at Darlington, he settled for third, and a late-race crash at the Charlotte Roval hampered his playoff run.

Larson's perseverance paid off in 2019 when he snapped a 75-race winless streak with a victory at Dover, propelling him to a sixth-place finish in the standings, his best to date.

In April 2020, Kyle Larson was suspended indefinitely by NASCAR and fired by Chip Ganassi Racing after using a racial slur during a livestreamed iRacing event. The incident sparked widespread backlash across the motorsport community and beyond.

The consequences were swift and severe: he lost key sponsors, his team ride, and his NASCAR eligibility. But unlike many in similar situations, Larson took responsibility. He publicly apologized, completed sensitivity training, and spent much of that year engaging directly with Black community leaders and diversity programs, including volunteering with the Urban Youth Racing School and The Sanneh Foundation.

He spoke openly about being the son of an interracial couple – his mother is Japanese and his father American – and how he disappointed himself.

Larson also returned to his roots – racing dirt tracks across America – and dominated. In late 2020, Rick Hendrick offered Larson a second chance and an opportunity with the legendary Hendrick Motorsports team for the 2021 season. Larson made the most of it.

Kyle Larson's 2021 season wasn't just a comeback – it was a masterclass. After sitting out most of 2020 in exile, he returned to NASCAR, with its most powerful team: Hendrick Motorsports. Hendrick didn't just give Larson a seat – he handed him the keys to the freshly resurrected #5 car and backed him with his own companies, HendrickCars.com and NationsGuard, while the rest of the corporate world played catch-up. Hendrick also gave Larson a rare green light to keep tearing up the dirt tracks, provided the main gig – the Cup Series – got top billing.

Kyle Larson's 2021 season wasn't just a comeback – it was a masterclass.

Larson hit the ground flying. A steady start at Daytona was followed by his first win with Hendrick three weeks later at Las Vegas, finally breaking his string of runner-up finishes on mile-and-a-half tracks. From there, the floodgates opened. He took out the Coca-Cola 600 in style, delivering Hendrick Motorsports its 269th Cup win – a new record, finally toppling the legendary Petty Enterprises. A week later, he dominated Sonoma for his first road course victory and then backed that up by winning the All-Star Race. Suddenly, the "comeback kid" had turned into a certified title contender.

Larson was unstoppable through mid-season. He nearly pulled off four wins in a row, only losing Pocono's first race that season on the final lap with a blown tire, then came back the next day, in a backup car, and finished second. That's Larson: punch him in the nose, he punches right back.

By Watkins Glen, he'd banked five wins and tied Denny Hamlin atop the standings. After Daytona, he officially locked down the regular season championship and entered the playoffs as the man to beat. At Darlington, he led 156 laps but settled for second.

What sets Larson apart from most of his peers is his versatility. He is arguably the most complete American race car driver of his era.

Then came the knockout punches: win number six under the lights at Bristol, a comeback win at the Charlotte Roval after battling electrical gremlins, and then Texas, where he became the first driver to lock into the Championship 4.

And he wasn't done. Kansas made it win number nine for the season, and for the second time that season, he'd won three races in a row. That hadn't been done since Dale Earnhardt's heyday. And then came Phoenix. The finale. Larson started on pole, led 107 laps, and when it mattered most, his pit crew delivered a lightning stop that vaulted him into clean air. He never looked back. Tenth win. First Cup championship. An emphatic exclamation point on a redemption arc that went from controversy to coronation in just over a year.

What sets Larson apart from most of his peers is his versatility. He is arguably the most complete American race car driver of his era. He competes in sprint cars, midgets, and late models – often against the best dirt racers in the world – and wins with impressive frequency. In 2021, he also claimed victory in the prestigious Chili Bowl Nationals, a crown jewel of dirt racing.

By 2022, Kyle Larson was no longer the comeback story – he was the benchmark. But as anyone in racing will tell you, staying on top is even tougher than getting there. The season began with promise: pole at Daytona, a win at Auto Club, and the kind of early pace that suggested another championship run was on the cards.

But racing gods are fickle. Sonoma turned ugly when a wheel departed the #5 car mid-race, earning his crew chief, Cliff Daniels, a four-week holiday courtesy of NASCAR. Watkins Glen delivered a second win, but mechanical gremlins and bad luck started stacking up. An early engine failure at Daytona. A spin and scrape at Darlington. A Round of 12 elimination after a rough day at the Roval. The title defense was over before the real fight began.

The Las Vegas tangle with Bubba Wallace also turned into more than just on-track drama. Contact with the wall led to a shoving match down the frontstretch and a rare one-race suspension for Wallace. Larson, ever composed, let the dust settle and did his talking at Homestead, winning for the third time that year and closing out

Kyle Larson celebrates in Victory Lane after winning the Pennzoil 400 at Las Vegas Motor Speedway in 2024. (Jeff Speer/LVMS/Icon Sportswire via Getty Images)

the season seventh in points. A solid campaign, but a reminder that nothing comes easy in the Cup Series, even for a generational talent.

The 2023 season started with another Daytona DNF – because of course it did – and by Phoenix, the #5 team was already in the headlines for the wrong reasons. A sneaky hood louver infraction triggered an L2 penalty: 100 points gone, playoff chances shaken, and Cliff Daniels suspended again. But the appeals panel eased the blow, restoring the points while keeping the fine and the ban. Larson responded like he always does – by winning. Richmond. Martinsville. Then the All-Star Race at North Wilkesboro, making him the first driver to win the

Kyle Larson (#32) was airborne in the Nationwide Series race at Daytona in 2013. (Alamy)

event at three different tracks. That put him in rare company alongside Dale Earnhardt and Jeff Gordon with three All-Star wins each.

Come playoff time, he lit it up again. He won the Southern 500, clinched Vegas to lock into the Championship 4, and gave the Hendrick engine department its 500th career win along the way. But the title chase came undone in Miami when Larson smashed into the sand barrels on pit entry, a rare but costly miscue. He finished the season second in points – a brutal pill, but no one questioned his speed.

Then came 2024. Larson opened steady with an 11th at Daytona, then turned up the heat at Las Vegas with

In 2024, Kyle Larson didn't just dabble in ambition – he went full throttle.

a commanding win. But Kansas stole the headlines – he beat Chris Buescher by 0.001 seconds, the closest finish in Cup Series history. That same year, Larson chased immortality by attempting "The Double" – racing both the Indy 500 and the Coke 600 on the same day. Rain delays meant he missed the start of the 600, handing the car to Justin Allgaier, but NASCAR granted him a playoff waiver, acknowledging that greatness sometimes breaks format.

He kept winning, too – Sonoma marked win 26, tying him with Dale Earnhardt Jr. and Fred Lorenzen. Then came the Brickyard 400 in July. Bristol followed with a jaw-dropping performance: 462 laps led out of 500, the most ever by a Hendrick driver in one race. That made it win number five for the year, and his 28th career victory, tying him with legends like Carl Edwards and Rex White. When he added another win at the Charlotte Roval, it looked like the championship was again in reach.

But at Martinsville, despite finishing third, the numbers didn't stack up. He missed the Championship 4 and wrapped up sixth in the standings. Still, six wins, more records, and more chapters added to what's shaping up as a Hall of Fame career.

In 2025, Kyle Larson didn't just dabble in ambition – he went full throttle. He lined up to take on motorsport's most daunting daily double again, the Indianapolis 500 and the Coca-Cola 600 on the same day. It was bold, brilliant, and pure Larson. Partnering with Arrow McLaren for his IndyCar debut, he crossed disciplines like it was just another Wednesday night sprint car show. And as expected, he looked right at home at 230 mph.

The only thing missing from his NASCAR resume is a Daytona 500 win.

Larson's legacy is already impressive with at least two Cup championships, multiple crown jewel wins, and a growing list of accolades across disciplines. But what makes his story so compelling is that it's far from finished. Whether it's more NASCAR titles, historic racing feats, or further boundary-breaking efforts in motorsports, Kyle Larson is still very much in the hunt – and still pushing the limits.

"Kyle's the modern-day Mario Andretti," Brown declared. "He can drive anything – dirt, asphalt, sprint cars, stock cars – and win. He's as close as we've got to those versatile legends like Andretti and A. J. Foyt."

IMMORTAL TEAM OWNERS

A handful of team owners have shaped the sport in ways that extend far beyond the checkered flag. Among the most influential are Raymond Parks, Carl Kiekhaefer, Junior Johnson, Richard Childress, Rick Hendrick, and Joe Gibbs – men who transformed garages into dynasties and drivers into legends. Though some began behind the wheel, their true legacies were written through their leadership, vision, and enduring impact on the teams they built.

RacingOne/Getty Images

Raymond Parks was NASCAR's first true team owner – and quite possibly its most intriguing. Long before Hendrick or Gibbs, Parks brought professionalism and polish to a ragtag world of bootleggers and backyard mechanics. He funded cars that won races and titles, including the first Strictly Stock (now Cup Series) Championship in 1949 with Red Byron behind the wheel.

Parks wasn't just a motorsport visionary but also a moonshine kingpin in Georgia's Prohibition-era underworld. His Atlanta-based liquor-running empire gave him the money, the muscle, and the mechanical edge to build fast cars and run faster than the law. He served time in federal prison for bootlegging, and his connections to the darker corners of Southern enterprise were well-known. Still, in NASCAR circles, Parks was revered. He cleaned up well, dressed sharply, and treated racing like big business long before the suits arrived. Without him, stock car racing might have stayed in the shadows – he helped bring it into the light, one fast car at a time.

Bryce Combs/ Wikimedia Commons

Carl Kiekhaefer, meanwhile, brought a level of dominance and innovation never before seen in the 1950s. The wealthy Wisconsin industrialist and founder of Mercury Marine entered NASCAR with a full-fledged factory-backed operation. His team won 16 consecutive races in 1956 – an unmatched streak – and captured back-to-back championships with Tim Flock and Buck Baker.

Kiekhaefer ran his team like a military unit, complete with strict dress codes and performance standards. He was demanding, but his results were undeniable. Despite withdrawing from the sport after two years, his impact on professionalism and team structure laid the groundwork for future team ownership models.

RacingOne/Getty Images

Junior Johnson's story is one of raw talent and deep roots. Born in the backroads of North Carolina, Johnson first gained notoriety as a moonshiner before becoming one of NASCAR's early stars. Though he won 50 races as a driver in the 1950s and '60s, it was his work as a team owner that truly set him apart.

After stepping out of the car, Johnson founded Junior Johnson & Associates and quickly became a dominant force in the Cup Series. He had an uncanny ability to recognize talent and a mechanical instinct few could rival. His most successful run came with Cale Yarborough, who delivered three consecutive championships between 1976 and 1978.

Johnson's second golden era followed with Darrell Waltrip, who brought home titles in 1981, 1982, and 1985, along with dozens of wins. Under Johnson's leadership, his team amassed 132 victories and established a reputation for excellence, tenacity, and innovation. Johnson operated on gut instinct and race-day intuition. He wasn't corporate. He wasn't polished. He was authentic, and that authenticity helped define NASCAR's modern era before he exited team ownership in the mid-1990s.

Chris Short/ Wikipedia Commons

While Johnson was the architect of NASCAR's old-school domination, **Richard Childress** emerged as the gritty builder of a new generation of stock car success. A journeyman driver through the 1970s, Childress wasn't winning races, but he was earning respect.

In 1981, he stepped away from the driver's seat and made a critical decision that would change NASCAR forever – he gave his car to Dale Earnhardt. Together, the pair became a legendary partnership. Earnhardt won six of his seven championships under the Richard Childress Racing (RCR) banner, turning the #3 Chevrolet into a fearsome presence on the track. While Earnhardt was the aggressive face of the operation, Childress was the steady hand guiding it.

The organization thrived through smart decision-making, mechanical consistency, and old-fashioned hard work. After Earnhardt's tragic death in 2001, Childress found new life through the rise of Kevin Harvick, who carried the team through the early 2000s with multiple wins. More recently, Childress's pairing with Kyle Busch has revived the competitiveness of the iconic team. RCR has now accumulated more than 100 Cup Series wins and remains one of the sport's most resilient and respected teams. Childress never strayed far from his roots, and his family-style operation continues to thrive in North Carolina – proof that loyalty, grit, and resilience never go out of style.

"I started out selling peanuts and popcorn at Bowman Gray in the '50s," said Childress. "Watching guys like the Myers brothers and Curtis Turner, I knew that's what I wanted. I bought a $20 taxicab – a '47 Plymouth – and started racing."

"Those were wild days," he added. "We'd go to Bowman Gray for a fight, and a race would break out. It was hard living – fast and rough – but I loved it."

He eventually made it to the Cup Series full time in 1973. "I worked two jobs, maybe dabbled in a little moonshine, but I always stayed within reason. I had to race to feed my family. I remember sending money back to my wife while I was on a two-month tour racing across the Northeast.

"I've been lucky to turn this into a business. But it's not for the faint of heart," Childress said. "When NASCAR shifted to the Next Gen car, we couldn't build everything. So, instead of laying people off, we launched new businesses. We're still hiring today."

As for his broader legacy, Childress is proud of the opportunities success has brought. "We've been able to support conservation work, travel the world, meet amazing people. But it all started with that $20 Plymouth and a dream."

Tom Pennington/Getty Images

As Childress was building RCR into a household name, **Rick Hendrick** quietly assembled what would become NASCAR's most successful team. A former drag racer and accomplished car dealer, Hendrick entered the sport in 1984 with All-Star Racing – a single-car team operating with minimal resources. But it was never just about racing for Hendrick. He saw NASCAR as an opportunity to combine business structure with motorsport performance, and it was this approach that laid the foundation for Hendrick Motorsports.

Hendrick's first breakout star was Jeff Gordon, who debuted in 1992 and ushered in a new era with four championships and 93 wins. Then came Jimmie Johnson, who delivered an unprecedented five straight titles from 2006 to 2010 and added two more in 2013 and 2016, matching the all-time championship record. Hendrick's team also fostered the careers of Terry Labonte, Chase Elliott, Kyle Larson, and William Byron, becoming the benchmark for excellence across generations.

With over 300 Cup Series wins and 14 championships, Hendrick Motorsports became more than a team; it became a standard. Hendrick introduced data-driven engineering, multi-car team dynamics, and a professional culture that elevated the sport. Through tragedy, including the heartbreaking 2004 plane crash that claimed 10 lives, including his son and key personnel, Hendrick remained a figure of strength. His ability to build winning teams and inspire loyalty across decades has made him arguably the greatest team owner in NASCAR history.

Mike Kalasnik/ Wikimedia Commons

While Hendrick was reshaping how NASCAR teams operated, **Joe Gibbs** was preparing to enter the sport with a different kind of pedigree. A three-time Super Bowl-winning coach with the Washington Redskins, Gibbs stunned the motorsports world in 1992 when he launched Joe Gibbs Racing (JGR).

Few believed an NFL coach could succeed in NASCAR, but Gibbs quickly proved his doubters wrong. Focusing on preparation, leadership, and team unity – principles that had defined his football success – Gibbs built a competitive and disciplined racing operation. The team won its first championship with Bobby Labonte in 2000 and then again with Tony Stewart in 2002 and 2005.

Gibbs's methodical approach and strong manufacturer backing from Toyota propelled JGR into the sport's top tier. The team's golden era came with Kyle Busch, whose tenure from 2008 onward resulted in two championships and over 60 wins. Denny Hamlin, a longtime JGR driver, also delivered consistent success with multiple victories and near-title seasons.

Under Gibbs, or "Coach" as his crew calls him, JGR expanded to four full-time cars and became a breeding ground for young talent like Christopher Bell and Ty Gibbs. With over 200 Cup Series wins and five championships, Gibbs demonstrated that leadership, no matter the sport, is about people, culture, and trust. His journey from the NFL to NASCAR is one of the most remarkable crossovers in professional sport, and his sustained success is a testament to his belief in process and preparation.

Together, Raymond Parks, Carl Kiekhaefer, Junior Johnson, Richard Childress, Rick Hendrick, and Joe Gibbs have overseen more than 800 Cup Series victories and more than 30 championships. But their influence cannot be measured solely in numbers. Each shaped the sport in his own way – Parks with structure, Kiekhaefer with dominance, Johnson with mechanical brilliance, Childress with hard-earned loyalty, Hendrick with business-minded innovation, and Gibbs with cultural leadership.

They mentored champions, adapted to changing eras, and navigated triumph and tragedy with resilience. In doing so, they didn't just build teams – they built NASCAR. Their stories are woven into the very fabric of the sport, and their legacies continue to guide it forward from pit road to podium.

Honorable Mentions

Many drivers have left their fingerprints on NASCAR's story – some chiseled into the stone of immortality, others hovering just shy of it. They didn't all rack up record stats or dominate year after year, but each brought something essential to the sport. For me, the closest calls – the drivers who nearly made the cut but sit just outside the inner circle – are Terry Labonte, Fireball Roberts, Junior Johnson, Fred Lorenzen, Curtis Turner, and Bill Rexford.

They're the "nearly" men or women. Drivers whose careers were built not just on wins or titles, but on timing, influence, style, and in some cases, unrealized potential. They may not be in the front row of NASCAR's Mount Rushmore – but they're standing right behind it.

Junior Johnson wasn't just a racer; he was a rebel alchemist, turning moonshine routes into racing lines. Before he won 50 races or revolutionized the sport as a team owner, he served 11 months in federal prison for running his father's still. The time behind bars only amplified the myth. Johnson didn't just break barriers – he detonated them, then rebuilt NASCAR in his own image. He may not have won a championship as a driver, but his legacy towers over the garage like a monument to Southern grit.

Terry Labonte was the opposite in almost every way – quiet, methodical, impossible to rattle. They called him "The Iceman" because he never got caught up in the noise. With 22 wins and two titles, he stitched together a career of quiet brilliance. His first championship in 1984 caught people off guard. His second, in 1996, came after a 12-year gap, the longest ever between titles. That alone is a flex few others could match. Labonte didn't need flash. He brought results, raced clean, and earned respect from the fiercest competitors – including Dale Earnhardt. He was never the loudest in the room, but he was always there at the end.

Fireball Roberts was the sport's original rockstar. The name alone still echoes. With 33 wins before his life was cut short in 1964, he was NASCAR's golden boy of the early superspeedway era – glamorous, fast, and sharp. He won the 1962 Daytona 500 and helped legitimize big-track racing. If fate hadn't intervened and taken his life, there's every reason to believe he'd be rubbing shoulders statistically with the all-timers. As it is, he remains one of the sport's biggest "what-ifs."

Fred Lorenzen brought polish and Midwestern charm to a sport still dripping with Southern red clay. Fast Freddie only raced full time for a handful of years, but he made it count – 26 wins, a Daytona 500, a pair of World 600s, and a win percentage during his prime that rivaled David Pearson's. He made NASCAR look good and helped it spread north of the Mason-Dixon line. Had he stuck around longer, we'd be talking about him in the same breath as the sport's heavyweights.

Curtis Turner was one of NASCAR's most charismatic and fearless pioneers, known as much for his flamboyant personality as his raw talent behind the wheel. A hard-charging driver and co-founder of the NASCAR Players Association, Turner competed in the sport's earliest decades, winning 17 races in the Cup Series between 1949 and 1965. Nicknamed the "Babe Ruth of Stock Car Racing," he was a master on dirt and paved tracks alike, and his skill in the cockpit was matched by his daring lifestyle off it. Despite being banned for several years in the early 1960s due to his efforts to unionize drivers, Turner returned to the sport and earned his final Cup victory in 1965 at Rockingham. His legacy is that of a bold, trailblazing figure whose contributions helped shape the rebellious spirit of early NASCAR.

And then there's **Bill Rexford** – a name that's been dusted over in history books, despite being the answer to a trivia question everyone gets wrong. He won the 1950 championship at just 23 years old, the youngest full-season champion for over 60 years. But injuries, inconsistency, and team changes saw him drift from the spotlight. Rexford never won again after that season and left the sport entirely within a few years. He was NASCAR's first champion to fade into obscurity rather than grow into greatness – a pioneer whose title should have been the start of a dynasty but ended up as a historical footnote.

Together, they make up NASCAR's "nearly" club – not quite immortalized like Earnhardt or Petty, but undeniably part of the DNA that built the sport.

No one beats an easy path into NASCAR, but some do it tougher than others. And while some names miss the statistical cut, their place in the story is undeniable, especially when you consider what they were up against.

Sara Christian wasn't just the first woman to race in NASCAR – she was on the grid for the very first Cup race in 1949. Seven starts, a fifth-place finish at Heidelberg, and a record that stood for more than 60 years. She didn't talk about diversity. She lived it.

Ethel Mobley took it further, lining up against her brothers, Tim, Fonty, and Bob Flock, on the sands of Daytona. Her career was brief, but symbolic. She wasn't there to make history. She was there to race.

Louise Smith brought chaos and charisma, racing hard and crashing harder. Eleven starts, a fearless spirit, and a reputation that outlived her stats. She once towed her wrecked car home just to prove a point – pure grit, pure NASCAR.

Then came the pioneers of color. **Elias Bowie**, the first African American to start a top-level NASCAR race in 1955, quietly showed up and turned laps at Bay Meadows. A year later, **Charlie Scott** drove for Carl Kiekhaefer at Daytona, the first Black driver to do so at that iconic track. Their records were short. Their impact wasn't.

Wendell Scott made it stick. Nearly 500 starts. Countless battles with underfunded equipment. And in 1964, a win that NASCAR tried to erase in real time, only to be rightfully restored in the history books. No gimmicks. No backing. Just raw courage and commitment.

And now **Bubba Wallace** carries that flame. His win at Talladega in 2021 made him the second Black driver to win at the Cup level, but his true power has been in using his platform to demand change – on racial justice, representation, and honesty in a sport long reluctant to face itself.

Then there are my personal favorites from the Antipodes, **Marcos Ambrose** and **Shane van Gisbergen**, both Immortals in Australian Supercars who chose to beat a different path.

The Devil Racer, **Marcos Ambrose**, brought his V8 Supercars fire and flair from Australia and quickly made a name for himself as a road course master, winning twice at Watkins Glen. He was raw, aggressive, and at times volatile, but when the track twisted and turned, Ambrose was as good as anyone in the field.

Years later, New Zealand's **Shane Van Gisbergen** stunned the NASCAR world by winning his Cup debut on the streets of Chicago in 2023. It was an instant classic; the kind of debut that made even hardened veterans sit up and take notice. Now he is a Cup Series driver with a diversity of talent that rivals Kyle Larson, but his career is just beginning in his mid-30s, not unlike the starting time for Lee Petty.

Benny Parsons embodied both grit and grace. The 1973 Cup champion, with his 21 career wins, wasn't flashy, but he was relentless. His title came with consistency, not dominance – he only won one race that year – but he was a fan favorite thanks to his easygoing personality and, later, his insightful commentary that helped grow the sport's TV presence.

Mark Martin is rated by many as the greatest driver to never win a Cup title. Five times a championship runner-up, Martin amassed 40 wins and the respect of every garage he entered. His clean driving style, fitness-first mindset, and loyalty made him a beloved figure across generations. He was also a prolific winner in the Busch Series and a key mentor to younger stars like Matt Kenseth and Carl Edwards.

Davey Allison had all the tools to become one of NASCAR's all-time greats – pedigree, talent, charisma, and guts. The son of Hall of Famer Bobby Allison, Davey emerged as the face of a new generation in the late '80s and early '90s, winning 19 Cup Series races in just over six full seasons. He nearly captured the 1992 championship, a year widely regarded as the most dramatic in NASCAR history, ultimately finishing third in a title battle decided in the final laps at Atlanta.

His rivalry with Kyle Petty and close bond with fellow rising star Alan Kulwicki added emotional depth to the era. Tragically, Davey was killed in a helicopter crash at Talladega Superspeedway on July 13, 1993, cutting short what could've been a legendary career.

Alan Kulwicki, meanwhile, was the definition of an outlier in NASCAR's big-money, multi-car world. A Polish-American mechanical engineer turned owner-driver, Kulwicki built his Cup Series team from scratch and outwitted the garage giants to win the 1992 championship.

He made headlines with his reverse "Polish Victory Lap" after his breakthrough win at Phoenix in 1988 – a symbolic gesture that became part of his mystique. Known for his fierce independence, meticulous engineering mind, and refusal to conform, Kulwicki's legacy rests on both his championship and its sheer improbability.

Tragically, he too died in an aviation accident – a plane crash in Tennessee on April 1, 1993, four months before Allison. Together, their deaths marked a heartbreaking end to a golden chapter in NASCAR's modern era.

Rusty Wallace brought a brash, bullish energy to NASCAR's modern era. The 1989 champion racked up 55 wins and became the face of the "blue-collar bad boy" archetype that defined the late '80s and early '90s. Wallace was fast, fearless, and never shy with his opinions, which made him a fan favorite – and a lightning rod.

Dale Jarrett, son of Ned, was a consummate professional and big-race ace. He won the Daytona 500 three times (1993, 1996, 2000) and secured the 1999 Cup title with Robert Yates Racing. Jarrett's calm, strategic approach paired perfectly with crew chief Todd Parrott's aggression, and he became one of the sport's most respected ambassadors during and after his driving career.

Matt Kenseth doesn't always get the spotlight, but his record speaks volumes. The 2003 Cup champion won 39 races and was the model of consistency. Ironically, it was his methodical title run – where he only won one race but led the points all season – that spurred NASCAR to overhaul the championship format the following year. In that sense, Kenseth didn't just win – he changed the sport.

Kasey Kahne was the heartthrob of the mid-2000s NASCAR boom, but his appeal went deeper than looks. He won 18 Cup races and could wheel a car with the best of them, especially on intermediate tracks. His popularity among fans and sponsors helped push NASCAR further into the mainstream.

Then there's **Martin Truex Jr.**, who transformed from journeyman to juggernaut. Long stuck in the midfield, he blossomed with Furniture Row Racing, winning the 2017 Cup title and becoming a perennial playoff powerhouse. His late-career resurgence is one of the best turnarounds in modern NASCAR, and his loyalty to small teams and underdog spirit made him a folk hero. Finally, we need to discuss Dale Junior.

Dale Earnhardt Jr. was NASCAR royalty by blood, but he came achingly close to carving his own name into the sport's pantheon of Immortals. A two-time Daytona 500 winner, fan favorite for over a decade, and a driver who carried the sport through some of its darkest and most transitional years, Earnhardt Jr. had everything – except a championship. That missing title is the one thread that keeps him just outside the inner circle of NASCAR's all-time greats.

His talent was undeniable, his impact immeasurable, but in a sport where championships are the ultimate currency, Junior was always a near-miss. He wasn't his father – and never needed to be – but that one elusive crown is what holds him at the doorstep of immortality, rather than firmly inside it.

Bibliography

Books

Branham, H.A. & Cain, Holly, *NASCAR Mavericks: The Rebels and Racers Who Revolutionized Stock Car Racing*, Motorbooks, 2024.

Charles River Editors, *Richard Petty: The Life and Legacy of The King of NASCAR*, Charles River Editors, 2020.

Crandall, Kelly, Creed, Jimmy, Hembree, Mike & Pearce, Al, *NASCAR 75 Years: The Official History*, Quarto Publishing Group, 2022.

Edwards, Fred K., *Richard Petty Biography: The Life and Legacy of a Motorsports Icon*, Independently Published, 2024.

Fielden, Greg & Auto Editors of Consumer Guide, *NASCAR: The Complete History*, Publications International, 2007.

Higgins, Tom & Waid, Steve, *Junior Johnson: Brave in Life*, David Bull Publishing, 1999.

Miller, Richard, *Bowman Gray Stadium*, Arcadia Publishing, 2013.

Pearce, Al & Hembree, Mike, *50 First Victories: NASCAR Drivers' Breakthrough Wins*, Octane Press, 2022.

Petty, Richard & Neely, Bill, *Grand National: The Autobiography of Richard Petty*, Henry Regnery Company, 1971.

Petty, Richard & Neely, William, *King Richard I: The Autobiography of America's Greatest Auto Racer*, Paperjacks, 1987.

Pierce, Daniel S., *Real NASCAR: White Lightning, Red Clay, and Big Bill France*, The University of North Carolina Press, 2010.

Thompson, Neal, *Driving With the Devil*, Three Rivers Press, 2006.

Wilkinson, Sylvia, *Dirt Tracks to Glory: The Early Days of Stock Car Racing As Told by the Participants*, Algonquin Books, 1983.

Yunick, Smokey, *All Right You Sons-a-Bitches, Let's Have a Race!*, Carbon Press, 2001.

Newspapers

Auto Action

Forbes magazine

Websites

Auto Action – autoaction.com.au

Cotton Owens Garage – https://www.cottonowens.com/

Fantasy Racing Cheat Sheet – frcs.pro/nascar

International Motorsports Hall of Fame – www.motorsportshalloffame.com

Motorsport Hall of Fame – www.mshf.com

NASCAR – www.nascar.com

New York Times – www.nytimes.com

North Carolina Sports Hall of Fame – ncshof.org

Secret Base Nation – www.sbnation.com

South Carolina Now – scnow.com

Speedway Media – speedwaymedia.com

The Official Tim Flock Homepage – www.timflock.com

The South Carolina Encyclopedia – www.scencyclopedia.org

The Virginian Pilot – www.pilotonline.com

Acknowledgments

Books like this don't just happen. They come together because people are generous with their time and willing to talk. In February 2025, I had the privilege of sitting down with Richard Petty, Richard Childress, and Drew Brown – three blokes who know a thing or two about racing – and they shared their stories and wisdom with the kind of openness that never stops surprising me.

But they weren't the only ones. NASCAR fans are a special breed – genuine, passionate, and usually happy to chat with a curious Aussie who turns up at race meetings asking all the "wrong" questions about long-past drivers and half-forgotten moments. If you've ever humored me in a paddock or at a pub near a track – thank you. This sport lives and breathes through its fans. They're the reason the money flows, the TV deals happen, and the sport stays alive. And I'll always make time for a chat.

There's no shortage of NASCAR books, which is a blessing and a curse. A blessing, because it gives writers like me a leg up. A curse, because it sets the bar high. But the sheer volume of writing on this sport tells you just how big it really is. It deserves every word.

Of course, some people in my life have to endure this madness. Byron and Gabi – my kids, now grown into impressive young humans – still lose out when I disappear into the research rabbit hole or spend weekends chasing stories, or weeks in the States. I don't say it enough, but I write for you two. And then there's Elaine – newer to my world, American by birth, blissfully indifferent to racing, but hopefully still willing to read every page.

Bruce at *Auto Action*, one of the sharpest motorsport people I know, probably hasn't realized how often I've picked his brain during all this. He does now. Thanks, mate.

And to the Gelding Street Press crew – you take my mess and turn it into a book. Raquel, Katie, and Brooke keep the wheels turning, while Vicky somehow gets these titles into people's hands and makes me look far more professional than I really am. Paul and Lisa, my team owners, thank you as well – this doesn't happen without the whole team.

So yes, it's got my name on the cover, but like every good race win, it took a hell of a crew to get here.

About the Author

Epic Photos/ Peter Norton

Writer Andrew Clarke loves sports – especially car racing and Aussie Rules football – and has been lucky enough to blend these loves with work. After starting his career as a football journalist he transitioned into motorsport and general motoring. He wrote his first book on the history of the Australian automobile, and has written a further 30 books on car races and racing and Australian Rules football. He has also ghostwritten autobiographies with seven athletes and personalities. Andrew has loved NASCAR racing since its days at the Calder Park Thunderdome and has published a NASCAR-focused magazine – *Rolling Thunder* – and twice raced in an Australian support series called Sportsman.

This is his third book for Gelding Street Press, with his first two being *The Immortals of Australian Football* (2024) and *Australian Football's 100 Year Club* (2025).

ad42.com.au
ad42media

ICHARD PETTY · DALE EARNHARDT · JIM
OHNSON · JEFF GORDON · LEE PETTY · D
EARSON · CALE YARBOROUGH · DARRELL
ALTRIP · TONY STEWART · JOEY LOGANO
BUCK BAKER · JOE WEATHERLY · HERB
HOMAS · TIM FLOCK · NED JARRETT · KY
USCH · RED BYRON · BOBBY ALLISON · B
LLIOTT · KYLE LARSON · RICHARD PETTY
ALE EARNHARDT · JIMMIE JOHNSON · JE
ORDON · LEE PETTY · DAVID PEARSON ·
ARBOROUGH · DARRELL WALTRIP · TONY
TEWART · JOEY LOGANO · BUCK BAKER ·
EATHERLY · HERB THOMAS · TIM FLOCK
ED JARRETT · KYLE BUSCH · RED BYRON
OBBY ALLISON · BILL ELLIOTT · KYLE LAR
RICHARD PETTY · DALE EARNHARDT · JI
OHNSON · JEFF GORDON · LEE PETTY · D
EARSON · CALE YARBOROUGH · DARRELL
ALTRIP · TONY STEWART · JOEY LOGANO
BUCK BAKER · JOE WEATHERLY · HERB
HOMAS · TIM FLOCK · NED JARRETT · KY

ICHARD PETTY · DALE EARNHARDT · JIM
DAVID PEARSON · CALE YARBOROUGH ·
OGANO · BUCK BAKER · JOE WEATHERLY
KYLE BUSCH · RED BYRON · BOBBY ALLIS
ETTY · DALE EARNHARDT · JIMMIE JOHN
EARSON · CALE YARBOROUGH · DARRELL
UCK BAKER · JOE WEATHERLY · HERB TH
RED BYRON · BOBBY ALLISON · BILL ELL
ARNHARDT · JIMMIE JOHNSON · JEFF GO
ARBOROUGH · DARRELL WALTRIP · TONY
VEATHERLY · HERB THOMAS · TIM FLOCK
OBBY ALLISON · BILL ELLIOTT · KYLE LAR
MMIE JOHNSON · JEFF GORDON · LEE PE
DARRELL WALTRIP · TONY STEWART · JO
ERB THOMAS · TIM FLOCK · NED JARRET
BILL ELLIOTT · KYLE LARSON · RICHARD
JEFF GORDON · LEE PETTY · DAVID PEAR
TONY STEWART · JOEY LOGANO · BUCK B
LOCK · NED JARRETT · KYLE BUSCH · REI
ARSON · RICHARD PETTY · DALE EARNHA
ETTY · DAVID PEARSON · CALE YARBORO